Reluctant
Hero

Reluctant Hero

A 9/11 Survivor Speaks Out About That Unthinkable Day, What He's Learned, How He's Struggled, and What No One Should Ever Forget

Michael Benfante
and Dave Hollander

Skyhorse Publishing

Skyhorse Publishing books may be purchased in bulk at special discounts for sales promotion, corporate gifts, fund-raising, or educational purposes. Special editions can also be created to specifications. For details, contact the Special Sales Department, Skyhorse Publishing, 307 West 36th Street, 11th Floor, New York, NY 10018 or info@skyhorsepublishing.com.

Skyhorse® and Skyhorse Publishing® are registered trademarks of Skyhorse Publishing, Inc.®, a Delaware corporation.

www.skyhorsepublishing.com

10 9 8 7 6 5 4 3 2 1

Library of Congress Cataloging-in-Publication Data is available on file.
ISBN: 978-1-61608-285-7

Printed in the United States of America

TO MY FATHER,

a perfect father to a child, a loving man to a son

TO MY MOTHER,

who loves me like a rock

CONTENTS

And we have seen our national character in eloquent acts of sacrifice. Inside the World Trade Center, one man who could have saved himself stayed until the end and at the side of his quadriplegic friend. A beloved priest died giving the last rites to a firefighter. Two office workers, finding a disabled stranger, carried her down 68 floors to safety. A group of men drove through the night from Dallas to Washington to bring skin grafts for burn victims.

In these acts and many others, Americans showed a deep commitment to one another and an abiding love for our country. Today, we feel what Franklin Roosevelt called, "the warm courage of national unity."

—President George W. Bush
Remarks at the National Day of Prayer and Remembrance,
September 14, 2001

And our hearts are full of gratitude for those who saved others. These men and women remind us that heroism is found not only on the fields of battle. They remind us that heroism does not require special training or physical strength. Heroism is here, all around us, in the hearts of so many of our fellow citizens, just waiting to be summoned—as it was on Saturday morning.

Their actions, their selflessness, also pose a challenge to each of us. It raises the question of what, beyond the prayers and expressions of concern, is required of us going forward. How can we honor the fallen? How can we be true to their memory?

—President Barack Obama
Speech at the memorial service for the victims of the shooting in
Tucson, Arizona, January 12, 2011

When I go home people'll ask me, "Hey Hoot, why do you do it man? What, you some kinda war junkie?" You know what I'll say? I won't say a goddamn word. Why? They won't understand. They won't understand why we do it. They won't understand that it's about the men next to you, and that's it. That's all it is.

—Black Hawk Down
From the screenplay by Mike Nolan, based on
the book by Mark Bowden

PREFACE: WHY THIS BOOK, AND WHY NOW?

THE WHOLE TOPIC of 9/11 is never a matter of small talk to me. It's no academic discussion. If someone casually says to me, "Hey, tell me your story," I tell them, "Nah, it's not going to work that way." But if somebody asks me, sincerely, "You were *that* guy? Can you talk about it?" Then I say, "Why don't you ask me questions, tell me what you want to know, and I'll tell you what I can." That's so much easier. I can handle that. Any other way is exhausting for me, and I don't want to do it.

To this day, it's impossible for me to give a summary explanation of how I really felt and what I really went through without telling everything—*every single thing* that I went through. I don't know how, psychologically, to tell someone an abbreviated version of what happened to me. People ask, and I say, "Yeah, I was there."

"Really?" they say.

Then they ask for more.

"Yes, I carried this woman down sixty-eight floors."

Then what? Then what?

It's a very intense and personal place to go. It takes a lot out of me. I don't like bringing it up. I don't go around telling people I carried a woman down sixty-eight flights in Tower 1 on 9/11.

"There I was, World Trade Center, September 11 . . ." This isn't the goddamn *World of Commander McBragg*.

Will I tell the story if asked? It depends on who's asking and what kind of emotional space they're coming from. But my story is not a cocktail party trick or somebody's cheap entertainment option.

Obviously, and for many reasons, it's an experience I now feel compelled to share with all seriousness, honesty, and emotion. But I can only tell it one way. That's from beginning to end, with nothing left out. And frankly, rarely are there times and places where that's an easy or appropriate thing to do.

Suffice it to say that I don't like telling this story. I don't even like thinking about it. For almost ten years I've stopped telling it altogether. And I've never really told the whole thing to anyone. That's hurt a lot of people. It's hurt me too. I want to tell it now. I need to tell it.

And I want to get it right. I will try hard—very hard—to tell it exactly like I remember it.

I'm still not sure I understand *it*—what it's meant, how it's changed me. Some call me a hero for it—for what I did on 9/11. I'm not very comfortable with that. What I do know is I need to tell everything to everybody (and I need to hear some things as well).

I know that if I retrace my steps, I can tell you how I came to be on the 81st floor of the World Trade Center, Tower 1, on 9/11, sitting at my desk at 8:46 a.m. when the first plane hit just twelve floors above me.

And then I spent the next ninety-six minutes inside Tower 1. I made it out, barely.

I was one of the lucky ones.

Sometimes I feel so awful about it I can't hear myself think a single thought. Other times I draw such hope and clarity from it. Either way, it's time to talk about it. So let me try here to tell you, and myself, what happened. Like I said, I will try hard to get it right.

INTRODUCTION: HOW DID I GET HERE?

I SAT HALF-DAZED, DOWNING beers and inhaling burgers at O'Reilly's Pub on 31st and Broadway. It was an unusual lunch at O'Reilly's for obvious reasons, but also because I was sitting in the back dining room. I'd eaten there a hundred times before, but I'd never sat in the back. That's usually where the "business people" had lunch, at the round tables with the white linen tablecloths. That's not where I usually sat. But this day it was sit there or sit nowhere. That's how crowded it was.

Boozer went to the bar to get more beers. I sat, fidgety, at a table with John. John wasn't saying much. Boozer yelled to me, "Raj!" (That's how they know me at O'Reilly's, after Roger Staubach.) He motioned for me to come to the front. "You gotta see this."

I came and I saw. It was me. On television. I couldn't believe what I was seeing. I really couldn't believe the camera guy made it out of there. But there I was: Lost and off-balance amid rubble, dust, and debris; rumpled light blue dress shirt, loosened navy blue tie; my black bag over my shoulder, a bottle of water in my left hand. I looked like hell.

The camera moved closer, and the questions started.

Cameraman: Who are you with?
Me: I was on the 81st floor.

My voice trembled slightly. Maybe only I noticed.

Cameraman: Tell me what you saw and heard.
Me: There were forty people in there. Just an explosion. I saw this light flash out my window. The whole doorway entrance to my office blew open. My office was freaking out. I just told them to calm down and get to the center of the office. Everybody was fine on my floor.

My voice was definitely shaky.
I'm shaky.

Me: We just started heading down the stairs. I heard people were trapped in the bathroom. I ran to the bathroom. It was just [*pause*] blown out. I asked if anybody was in there. People weren't in there. So I started going down the steps. I heard people shouting. I stopped at, like, sixty-eight; and there was a woman in a wheelchair, and I got her in the straps—the wheelchair—and I carried her down the steps. Carried her down sixty-eight floors, man. [*Coughs.*] Then we got lost on the 5th floor. It was chaos.

Cameraman: Who do you work for?
Me: Network Plus, a communications company out of Randolph, Massachusetts.

Cameraman: How do you spell your name?
Me: Mike Benfante. B-E-N-F-A-N-T-E.

I couldn't reconcile it—the reality of where I'd just been and the comparative normalcy of O'Reilly's. For a moment I felt the fear from before, from down there. Dryness crept up the back of my throat. Out of the corner of my eye, I could see Boozer staring at me. I felt more eyes on me from all around the bar. Somebody patted me on the back. I looked up. I was still on television.

On the TV the camera stayed with me as I walked toward John. I grabbed his arm, and we circled for a moment, disoriented, trying to get our bearings. I muttered to no one in particular, "It's chaos, man. It's chaos."

As we walked out of the frame, the camera surveyed the devastation behind us, slowly focusing its lens toward the top of the North Tower, where smoke streamed from the upper floors. Abruptly, the segment cut to the tower imploding, capturing full audio of the deliberate deep, rumbling sound. Next they cut to a hand wiping dirt from the camera lens, revealing a clear ground-level shot of me running—*running for my life*—full-speed toward the camera, John running behind me, and a ferocious cloud of white dust coming up fast behind us, enveloping everything in its path. Debris flying, voices crying out. People swept off their feet into the air. You could hear the sounds of large objects and particles scraping against the cement ground, against metal signs, and against vehicles. The white dust consumed the entire television screen. Then blackness. Blackness and silence. I'll never forget that blackness.

You can't really plan where you're going to be on the worst day of your life. And it's hard to imagine that the worst day of your life might also be one of the worst days in modern history. Long before that day, I had plans. I had goals. But none of them included being in the World Trade Center on September 11, 2001.

PART I

A JERSEY GUY

FRIDAY, SEPTEMBER 7, 2001

I didn't love my Jersey City studio apartment on 234½ 7th Street. It was small and dumpy, but I got a great deal on it. Joy lived right across Hamilton Square Park. I called her before heading out the door for the train. I'd pick her up after work. We'd get dinner, or maybe see a movie. We had a lot to talk about. Two weeks earlier, after an entire summer of searching, we'd finally found a place to have our wedding. The big event was a year away, but there was plenty to do right away. Life wasn't simple. Still, I was looking forward to the weekend. Forecasts called for sun, blue skies, highs in the low eighties. Maybe we could go down to the Shore? There were so many plans.

My plan—my big plan—always included living in northern New Jersey. That's where I'm from. That's where my family is. That's where I've always wanted to end up. As a kid, I skinned my knees in the parks and playgrounds of Montclair, Verona, and Bloomfield. I earned all-conference football and track honors at Immaculate Conception High School. Except for four years spent at Brown University, and cup of coffee here and there, I've lived in New Jersey all my life.

In fact, that's what I told Network Plus. I wanted to be in New Jersey. "Someday you'll be able to open your own New Jersey office." That was their big speech to me at my interview. They painted a pretty picture. But when I woke up on Friday, September 7, 2001, I was headed into Network Plus offices in

New York City, on the 81st floor of the Word Trade Center's North Tower. I sold telecommunications there. To be precise, I managed others who sold telecommunications. That's what I did.

I'd been working for Network Plus since May 1994. I didn't plan on that, either. I graduated from Brown in 1987; months later, the market crashed, and any prospects I had of becoming an investment banker crashed with it. I settled for commercial banking, but that didn't do it for me. I wanted out of banking. Sales, in most any field, sounded like the right direction. It just happened to be telecom sales.

My rise through Network Plus wasn't a straight line. While living in Princeton, New Jersey, I cut my teeth for two years at their office in nearby Bluebell, Pennsylvania. It was a new office, and Network Plus was a fairly new company, founded only three years earlier, in 1991. In 1996, they sent me down to Springfield, Virginia, to resuscitate a floundering sales office. The move was a disaster. The office was poorly positioned geographically, making recruitment nearly impossible. I tried hard for ten months, but the office never took off. When a sales manager position became available in Norwalk, Connecticut, I jumped all over it. Connecticut wasn't the biggest sales region, but it was a helluva lot bigger than Springfield; and I got to manage a sizable sales staff. The Network Plus home office was based relatively nearby in Randolph, Massachusetts. Most importantly, it was a step closer to being back in New Jersey. The company was expanding. Network Plus was building a network, becoming a competitive local exchange carrier, a CLEC as it's called in the trade. They opened up additional offices, and finally, they asked me to find office space in New Jersey. Things were looking up.

I quickly found suitable space and negotiated a favorable lease. All we needed to do was sign. But Network Plus put the brakes on the transaction. They were already setting up an office in New York City. "It makes no sense to open up a New Jersey office too," they explained. To say I was disappointed would be an understatement.

Adding insult to injury, the New York office already had a sales manager. And they had already filled my old position as sales manager at the Norwalk office. This meant I'd go from being the manager of my own office to an assistant manager in New York City. This was not my plan. I had already reached my personal goal of becoming the sales manager of an office. That was big for me. "Assistant manager" meant I was back out there selling. That was difficult for me. The thing is, I'm a better sales manager than I am a salesman. I don't get jazzed about all the little details that make a top salesman—bringing in doughnuts, remembering birthdays, sending out Christmas cards. I respect those professional traits in others. It's just not my cup of tea. For me, going back to selling was like being a detective being told to walk a beat again. It felt like I was taking a step back.

September 3, 1998, on my first day at the New York City offices, I looked around and saw we had only six salespeople. It would be an uphill battle. Still, I was in downtown Manhattan, in a spectacular office space on the 81st floor of one of the world's most famous buildings, the World Trade Center. How bad could life be? Within a year, the manager of the New York City office was promoted to regional manager, and I took over his job. And things took off for me.

New York City turned out to be a perfect fit. I performed better in all aspects of my job. I liked the city. I liked riding the subway. I loved recruiting talent. Most of the salespeople I hired were from the New York area, but I also recruited young sales-people from all over the country who were either new to New York or fresh out of college. That kind of recruiting was a first for Network Plus. At the height of our operation, we had forty salespeople in the New York office.

I was having a great time. I was active. I personally took every hire under my wing and out on their first sales calls. I gained a lot of respect from my salespeople for being in the trenches with them. People knew what they had to do. My guys and I were in sync. Business was booming.

My office quickly emerged as one of the company's top two sales offices. Network Plus eventually opened an office in New Jersey and offered it to me. But I didn't want it. I had New York City.

*   *   *

I loved Fridays for many reasons, but Friday, September 7, felt especially nice. We were a week past Labor Day, and it was still perfect beach weather. Just before I descended underground to the Port Authority Trans-Hudson train, Joy called me on my cell phone. "Let's definitely do a movie tonight," she said. "It'll be good to give ourselves the night off from wedding planning." She was right. "What if we got up early and went to the Shore tomorrow?" she said. The girl could read my mind. I hadn't even gotten on the train, and I was already looking past my day at Network Plus. I said I'd call her from the office, later on. You see, that was the other thing about moving to the World Trade Center office. It's where I met Joy.

Not long after I arrived at Network Plus's New York office, in April 1999, I served as best man at Jeff Fernandez's wedding in Key West. I flew down on a Tuesday. Jeff got married that

Saturday. I left on Sunday. It was like spending a week at Mardis Gras with a wedding thrown in. What a party.

I'd known Jeff's entire family since meeting them my freshman year at Brown, sixteen years before. My fraternity nickname at Brown was *Harry*, after Harry Belafonte. My last name is *Benfante*, which sounds similar to *Belafonte* (creative bunch, those Ivy Leaguers). So this group knows me as Harry. They also know I was one of the last of my college friends to remain single. So all the mothers and wives dug in: Harry, when are you going find a nice girl? Harry, when are you going settle down? Harry, when are you going to get married? Unable to take the pressure any longer, I cried out, "The reason I'm not married yet is because I'm making sure my friends are taken care of first. It's been hard enough setting these guys up one by one with the right girls, this weekend's groom included. Starting Monday, I'll worry about myself." Mercifully, this ended the inquisition.

When I got back to the office on Monday, I noticed a new girl. She was the assistant to the vice president on the local network side of the business. I'll never forget walking into the office that day and seeing her for the first time—sitting there at her cubicle with perfect posture in front of the computer, wearing a white shirt under a sleeveless navy blue dress, gorgeous long black hair. I thought she was so beautiful. Later that week, I was having a conversation with a co-worker about Ayn Rand novels. I couldn't remember the name of the protagonist in *The Fountainhead*, and the new girl, seated two cubicles away, just blurted out, "Howard Roark." I was very impressed. (To this day she says I shot her a dirty look, but really, it was one of delighted surprise. *Really*.) That was the first time I ever spoke with Joy Osuna.

For the next two months, we saw each other in passing, and that was about it. Sometimes I asked her to write reports or clean up a document. Admittedly, I was overly critical of her work. (A not-so-subtle way of getting her attention, she claims.)

And then it happened. On a random Thursday night, June, 17, 1999, John Powers, a college buddy of mine who lived in Connecticut, phoned late in the afternoon to say he was in the city, and could we have a drink? We arranged to meet at Bryant Park. I packed myself up and headed toward the elevator. On my way out I whizzed by Joy, who was chatting with another senior administrative assistant. Though my feet kept moving, my mind hesitated. I knew she lived uptown, which theoretically had us heading in the same direction. As I stepped into the elevator, I thought, somewhat impulsively, *Why don't I ask her if she would like to take the subway ride together?* I caught the closing elevator doors with my foot, got out, and walked back into the office. And I asked her.

After registering slight shock, she said yes, and I waited for her to get ready. We took the subway uptown. The ride was kind of awkward at first. I only meant it as a friendly invitation. Well, maybe I did. Sure, she was cute, and I was attracted to her. Still, I wasn't thinking about much more than going to meet a friend and maybe getting to know her a little bit better in the process.

We got to Bryant Park, and after one drink my buddy John Powers had to get back home to Connecticut. I turned to Joy, awkwardly, and managed to come out with "Are you hungry?" She said yes. So off we went to a kind-of-charming Italian restaurant in the Turtle Bay section of town—2nd Avenue and 53rd Street—called Caffe Buon Gusto.

A waitress led us upstairs to the nicest little table for two overlooking the avenue. It was very romantic. The menus came, and it struck both of us at the same time that, well, this is like a date. Awkward moment number three. To break the uncomfortable silence, I joked, acting as if I were the big shot on an official first date, "Order anything you like on the menu." We tossed each other a playful look and a half smile, thinking the same thing: *Sure, OK, why not? Let's see how this goes.*

After a wonderful dinner, we moved to a lively bar next door. We had drinks and watched the Knicks play San Antonio in the NBA Finals. The Knicks won!

From there we went to another place, and from there another and from there another. We ended up at a New Orleans–themed bar called Harglo's across 2nd Avenue and a few blocks down from Caffe Buon Gusto. It was around 2:00 a.m., and we were having a blast. The bar was owned by a charming old woman named Cia and her gregarious Greek family. I told Cia that it was Joy's birthday (Joy's real birthday was a week before, but hey). She brought out a piece of chocolate cake with a candle in it. It was the sweetest thing you ever saw. Joy blew out the candle, and then we clapped for her—me, Cia, her family, and two other customers. The jukebox played Sinatra's "I've Got You Under My Skin." I love that song. I know every word. I grabbed Joy, and we started dancing, me singing in her ear.

Cia asked how we got together. She asked all about us. She had us laughing. I went to the bathroom; then Cia and Joy got to talking. Cia asked Joy, "How do you know dis man?"

Joy said, "I don't know him so well, he's a co-worker. We're out for the first time."

"He is a very good man—handsome," Cia said.

"You think so?" said Joy, making Cia laugh.

"Listen to me," Cia said, drawing Joy closer. "I think you gonna to marry dis guy."*

---

*Almost exactly two years later, I returned to Harglo's, got down on one knee, and, with Cia as my witness, proposed marriage to Joy.

On cue, I came out of the bathroom and rejoined Joy at the bar. I started telling her story after story, semi-nervously trying to keep her entertained and probably thinking too much about how great this was all feeling and how it was all going. And then, in the middle of my talking about God-knows-what, out of nowhere, she kissed me. Stunned, and overthinking the situation, instead of kissing her back, I just picked up the conversation where I left off, practically in midsentence. But as she pulled away and gracefully resumed listening to my tales of glory, I saw something in her—something so lovely and familiar.

All your life you hear couples talk about that magic night where you spill your guts and bond with that special someone. That night was it for me and Joy. We didn't want to go home.

The next day at Network Plus, at 8:30 a.m., Friday, there was an unscheduled, mandatory all-staff meeting on sexual harassment in the workplace. We both attended and took copious notes.

That was the heady summer of 1999. I was thirty-four, and for the first time in years I felt that things were coming together for me. I met Joy. I found my own place in Jersey City. Just a few months later, in January 2000, I became manager of my company's World Trade Center office that was rocking, staffed with great people I had trained. And all the while, I knew that Network Plus was going public. In my mind, the whole point was to go public and cash in those stock options. That was the pot of gold at the end of the rainbow. That's what I was working for. And I had worked hard to get myself to that position. When Network Plus went public in June 1999, it was the high point of my professional career. The stock rose every day. I really felt that I had accomplished something not only as a manager, but also financially, for myself.

Not so fast. A few months later, in the fall of 1999, the dot-com/telecom crash hit New York. Network Plus crashed right along with it. Because of my quick rise through management and my relatively long tenure at the company, I had a lot of stock options. Not only did I have the options, but I also had some on margin that I didn't cover. I also had some of my retirement money reinvested in the stock. I had a lot of money invested in Network Plus. By December 2000, it was over. I'd lost everything.

I had been with the company for seven years. The whole reason I stayed—the pot of gold—was gone. There I was, interested in this girl, thinking I'm financially secure, thinking that now is a good time to get serious in a relationship. I told Joy I was financially secure. Now I felt like an idiot. The one thing I was riding on was gone. I thought, *Now where are you? You're in a job—with no pot of gold at the end of the rainbow. You're just living for your paycheck and a commission.*

What could I do?

There was this idea about debt restructuring, in which you try to build the stocks back up and hope they rebound. But it was like throwing good money after bad. Things got worse. I sat in on meetings, listening to one comeback strategy after another—we'll do this, then do this, become "EBITDA positive"—and it was all bull. We knew it. My CEO was a very charismatic salesman. The way he put it was, "Be a good soldier." I could relate to that. It gave some meaning to things, I guess.

Was I resentful? Was my team? A lot of things were said and done that could've been handled differently and would've had a better impact on the employees and the people who had invested their time in the company. Let's face it, there were certain owners who cashed in at some point. We were reading every day about dot-com and telecom owners cashing in on smoke-and-mirrors companies. Despite it all, I tried to keep things positive. I devised a personal comeback strategy and set new goals: grow my sales force to fifty people, make a mark as a sales manager in the telecom industry, build a résumé.

Our office was still having fun. We were an excellent sales force. We met our quotas. We set additional goals and met them too. There was always a bonus at the end of the month. The home office would throw me a couple thousand dollars, and I'd always tell my guys that if they reached such and such goal, it was open bar for the night. We had a lot of good times. We bonded over work and play. We were a solid core of people who looked out for each other. It was a real team. I was no longer sure I liked the telecom industry, but I liked being a manager. I liked showing people how to sell. I liked watching people become successful and helping them get there. The people were what kept me going.

Joy and I continued dating without anybody at Network Plus knowing about it. Although relationships in the workplace are fairly common these days, we felt more comfortable exercising discretion. Even after May 2000, when Joy took a new job with Atlantic Records, we still kept our relationship quiet. Also around that time, Joy moved into a studio across from my apartment near Hamilton Park in Jersey City. I've never had a friendlier neighbor.

While riding the PATH to work that Friday, September 7, I began wishing we had played hooky and went down to the Shore a day early. Instead, I cracked open a book. A lot of us in the office were readers. We regularly swapped books. It was a diverse group of young people, so you got a bit of everything. And there were times when the whole office was reading different books by one author. That weekend I was reading *Black Hawk Down* by Mark Bowden, the true story about our policing action in

Somalia, where thirteen U.S. soldiers were killed in what was supposed to be a routine mission. This book floored me. It was inspiring, gut wrenching, smart. It described in graphic and painstaking detail how, through camaraderie and teamwork, a unit of soldiers overcame tremendous adversity in the face of deadly conditions. I swapped for it earlier that week and couldn't put it down. I actually wished my PATH ride lasted a little longer so I could continue reading.

Friday was an "out day" at the office. In our typical sales week, Monday and Thursday were "in days," when you set your appointments over the phone; and Tuesday, Wednesday, Friday you were out selling—out days. Friday, September 7, marked the first week into a new selling month, so without immediate pressure to meet monthly quotas hanging over our heads, things weren't too hectic.

Friday is a great selling day. Prospects usually have things cleared off their desks. They're in a good mood. It's a great day to bring home business.

On out days my team worked like a well-oiled machine. I paired my core of twenty veterans with mid-level salespeople. I took all the new trainees, going out in front of people and showing them how to sell. That morning, I went out with Marc Reinstein. Marc wasn't a trainee, but sometimes it was just good to get out. I had hired Marc in the spring of 2000 when he was a year or two out of college. A lot of people didn't want to hire him, but I saw something in Marc, which proved to be right. He ended up being a very good salesman. He and I had a good out day that day.

That Friday, like all Fridays, we ended the day at 5:00 p.m., earlier than the usual 6:00 p.m. out time for the rest of the week. It wasn't a requirement to come back to the office on an out day, but a lot of people did. The main reason most people came back was to convene at the nearby John Street Bar & Grill. It was our weekly ritual. That Friday night was no different.

I stayed later at John Street than I had planned. That wasn't unusual. Feeling guilty, I called Joy. "Do you still want to see a movie?" She wasn't sure. Maybe we should go to dinner first, then see a movie. Or maybe we should stay in. Both of us were trying to find the right activity where we could keep our minds guilt-lessly off our wedding planning while not completely ignoring it.

SATURDAY, SEPTEMBER 8, 2001

Joy and I got engaged on June 8, 2001. We spent much of that summer trying to find the right place to get married. It wasn't easy. We wanted to get married outdoors. We wanted the place to ourselves. We wanted something special, something different; and most of all, we wanted what we wanted. Joy was becoming very discouraged. Nothing was right. The last week in August, we found the Pleasantdale Chateau in West Orange, New Jersey. Joy loved it. But it cost too much—much more than we wanted to spend. After so many rough outings, my fiancée was close to tears. We asked for a Saturday in September 2002. All the Saturdays were booked. Then we asked for a Friday. All Fridays were booked. I could see Joy was at her breaking point. "Actually," the property manager said, "there is a Friday open. Are you superstitious?" He gave us a great deal for Friday, September 13, 2002.

It had only been two weeks since we signed the contract for the wedding reception with Pleasantdale Chateau, and already we had a to-do list a mile long. We decided that the best thing to do was to give ourselves the day off. We knew the weather on Saturday was going to be exceptionally nice, so we got up early and drove an hour down the Garden State Parkway to Spring

Lake, a storybook-pretty town on the New Jersey Shore. I spent the day with my head buried in *Black Hawk Down*. The book got me so wound up that I'd stop reading, hand the book to Joy, and have her read a passage out loud so we could talk about it. Time flew.

We drove home around 6:00 p.m. We cruised up the Parkway sun-drenched and sandy, windows down and the wind in our hair, blasting Lou Reed's "Perfect Day" on the stereo.

That night we had dinner at Katie Ryan's. We'd been meaning to go there for some time. It's an older, pub-style joint that's been a favorite in Jersey City for ages. We sat upstairs and ordered steaks. It was well worth the wait. The food was top notch, and the atmosphere swelled with old Jersey City soul.

I've always cherished my weekends. This really was a perfect day.

SUNDAY, SEPTEMBER 9, 2001

All my life, I've been going to my parents's house for Sunday dinner. That's where Joy and I went that Sunday. We watched football. We played in the yard with my nieces and nephews. We ate and ate and ate. My family is the central, most important thing in my life.

We're a close family that doesn't like to be too far from each other. I grew up in Montclair, New Jersey, with my entire family living under one roof: my parents, my siblings, and my grandparents. The house was sold in 1999. Then my sister and my parents found what's known as a "mother-daughter" house in Verona about a half mile from my younger brother, Angelo, who was already living there with his family. So it became Sunday dinner at my "parents and sister's house"—the family place.

I'd really love for you to picture it. You've got the kids running around. It's a loud family dinner table—lots of joking and heated debates on all kinds of subjects. We get into typical Italian-American, voices-raised "I'm always right and you're definitely wrong" discussions. Topics range from who was a better running back, "Walter Payton or Jim Brown?" to the classic "Somebody says you said something, but you say you didn't." Or it could be something about how to raise the kids. The men always have some criticism about the food when they don't know how to cook themselves. There's never a dull moment, I assure you.

That particular Sunday, we gathered with renewed family excitement because it was the first Sunday of the NFL season. The Giants were scheduled to play on Monday night, so we watched the Jets. We are decidedly a family of Giants and Yankees fans. It's serious business for us.

We're serious about food too. My mother does the cooking, and my sister Maria does the desserts and baking. They're both incredibly talented. We serve a four-course meal: First plate is always pasta with gravy. In the gravy you have sausage, meatballs, a little pork; or sometimes my mom might break out the special family recipe, "eggs in the gravy," or, on an extra special occasion, beef braciole. (By the way, real Italians—at least real Italians where I grew up—call gravy what most people call tomato sauce.) A bowl of ricotta cheese and a fresh block of pecorino romano floats from person to person throughout the meal. The second plate is usually roasted chicken with a salad, which often includes a sideshow of my father and me fighting over the roasted liver in the oven pan. The third plate is fruits and nuts, especially almonds. We're crazy for our almonds. And the fourth plate is one of Maria's amazing desserts. She makes cookies, cream puffs, chocolate cake; and quite often she makes a cheesecake with my favorite—everybody's favorite—roasted almond crust. (Maria's desserts are so legendary that we've often talked about opening a business for her. She says, "If I had to do it for money—not love—I wouldn't do it.") We top it all off with espresso and sambuca. My friends, the entire experience is even better than it sounds.

We usually begin eating right as the first football game is ending, around 4:30 p.m. When we're all around that table, it's the most comfortable place in the world for me. When you look at my family, you can really see me. It's not complicated. I am the son of a hardworking, loving Italian-American family. My paternal grandparents were born in Sicily. Both came here as teenagers in the early 1900s. My grandfather was a typical old-school greenhorn, strict with no debate. He spoke broken English. He never got a driver's license. What he knew, and knew well, was how to work. He worked as a construction laborer and was a charter member of the laborer's union Local 694 in Montclair. He arranged for me to be a provisional member so I could work jobs during my summers home from college. As a boy, I often helped him cut the lawn or work in the garden. Whatever he busied himself with around the house, I helped him. He loved that.

He was a tough old bastard, my grandfather. Let me give you an indication of how tough. He got hit by a car when he was sixty-five, shook it off, and lived to eighty-six. "Just a bruise," he would say.

I've always enjoyed a close relationship with my father. He lived for his kids. He was there for whatever you needed—a ride, advice, help of any kind. He also lived vicariously through his kids, especially with sports, which was a major part of my youth. Like his father, he was a laborer. He used to cut out from a job in New Jersey on a Friday at noon to catch my 4:00 p.m. freshman football games at Brown in Rhode Island. And although I was very active in sports, he was never one of those dads who insisted that their kid play a certain sport or do a certain thing. He let us do our own thing. My father and I have never been the type to say "I love you" all the time. But if I could paint you a picture of what love looks like, you'd see me standing next to my dad.

My mom is the typical protective, worrying, wants-to-wash-your-underwear-cook-all-your-meals-all-the-time Italian mother. Raised in Brooklyn, she is one of four sisters. Her father, James Terzano, had light hair and enjoyed his drink, so everybody called him Jimmy Irish. He died young, when my mother was just about to get married. My maternal grandmother died when I was five. I remember her as a sweet woman who lived out on Long Island with my mother's younger sister.

My mother loves children. She's coddling and protective almost to a fault. It's as if she doesn't want them to see the realities of the world until they have to, and if she could prevent that from happening, she would. I used to tell her, "Mom, sooner or later we have to face the music in life, and you want your children to be prepared for it." As a kid, I sensed her protectiveness, so I walked that line, pleasing her but experiencing the world as much as I could.

When it came time for my parents to drop me off at my freshman dorm, I didn't think it was a big deal. But it was a big deal for my mom. I was the first in our family to leave home and the first to graduate college. (It helped that in high school I made all-county football and track, became an honors student, and was recruited by Brown to play football.) After we said our good-byes, my dad came back up to my room because my mother forgot something. "Why didn't Mom come back up?" I wanted to know. She was crying in the car, that's why. And it dawned on me then how much it meant to her, keeping the family together. The family unit remains the most important thing in the world to my mother.

She wrote me letters at college all the time. I still have them. There's nothing better than getting a letter when you're at school. My mother always gave me support and encouragement. She senses better than anyone what's going on with me—even when I don't know what's going on with me, which is more often than I'd like. She knows when to knock you down and pick you up. She's the best at picking me up. My mother knows I don't make all the right decisions in life, but she's not too critical. Still, she lets me know just what she's thinking.

When I announced my engagement to Joy, I thought my mother would be thrilled. I was thirty-six years old with a long history of relationships that had gone nowhere. Some had met the family, but most didn't. So how did my mother react to the news that her oldest son was finally settling down? "Know what you're doing here," she said to me. "Don't mess around—for *her*, and for you. Don't be a jackass." My own mother was asking me what my intentions were.

I didn't exactly make it easy on my parents all the time. During my teen years, I was a bit of a hell-raiser. I got into a lot of trouble in and out of school. Half the teachers loved me, and half resented me. I was making national honor roll during the week and getting into huge brawls over the weekend.

My parents couldn't choose my friends any more than I could choose my family. But the friends I chose, no matter how they might have looked like to outsiders, carried—at their core—a code of values that made sense to me. I know in my heart that if it was one of those guys who found themselves on the 68th floor in Tower 1 on 9/11, they would've done no different than I did, and you would've read about one of them in the papers and seen them on *Oprah* instead of me. Not one of those guys would have left anybody behind. How do I know? Because that's the way we were with each other. Maybe we did get into trouble—

but we were in it together. When one was in trouble, all were in trouble. I'm talking about the Lever brothers, Mike and Rick (we called them Ike and Clever), the Michura brothers, Paul and Luke (Nips and Louie), and the McKeown brothers—Bob, Tom, and Paul (Bull, Tom, and Mac). They were all older than me. We played football together in Pop Warner and high school. And that led to other stuff. But whatever it was we got into, it was always backed by an all-for-one-and-one-for-all code. If each of us is made up of where we've been in this life, then who I was and what I did on 9/11 surely had something to do with those boys. And maybe my parents knew that about me and them, and knew we were worth the "trouble."

My parents knew when to let the reins go and when to pull them back. They struck the right balance with me, because truth be told, I was the type of kid who could've gotten into a lot more trouble than I did. They gave me an unconditional love that let me know I could always go home. And I always wanted to.

That's what's most important, I think: *wanting* to be with your family. No matter how lost you get running with the fast crowd, partying or thinking that you're somebody you're not, you'll be OK if you find solace and safety in the desire to return home. As they say, "There's no place like home." My mother and my father made it like that, for me and each of my three siblings.

My brother, Angelo, is two and a half years younger than me. He is my youngest sibling. When we were teenagers, I tried to keep some distance because I didn't want him to run with my crowd. We grew extremely close as adults. Angelo got married before I did. He and his wife, Lisa, had two children, my niece Amanda and my nephew Angelo Jr., who is also my godson.

Nobody has a bigger heart than my big sister Maria. She'll do anything for you. Wherever she's worked, whatever group she's involved in—they all love Maria. Like my mother, she lives for her kids. She and her husband, Marc, have three children: MarcAnthony, Sara and Angelina, and I marvel at how much love she gives her family day in and day out.

Susan is my oldest sister. She has Down syndrome. We had to look out for her.

In many ways, with Susan, it was always like having a younger sister. This is another thing about my parents. When Susan was born in 1959, they didn't know as much about Down syndrome and other disabilities as they do today. Back then, parents were often advised by doctors to institutionalize the child. Susan was born premature. She lay in the hospital incubator, very tiny, and my father would visit every day. When he put his hands into the rubber gloves and held Susan through the incubator, he said, "I don't care what those doctors say. She's coming home, and she's going to live with us." And that's where Susan lives to this day.

Your home can be a place where you learn fundamental values. My home taught me love for all kinds of people no matter how different they may be. It taught me to value and respect each individual. We take care of each other. We don't give that responsibility over to others. This gave me a special insight and awareness. I always knew. I didn't have to be told. I was protective to a fault sometimes. I got into a few scrapes with people who aren't as sensitive and not as understanding. You know how kids are.

I remember attending events at Susan's school for disabled children, with Maria and Angelo. We used to run around with all these kids with Down syndrome or autism or whatever. We had a blast. Some people get a little skittish around disabled people—*people like that.* I just treat them like anybody else. As a result, everybody has fun.

As siblings go, we grew up literally closer than most. Angelo and I shared the same room until we went to college. Our twin beds were so close together we could stretch out our arms and practically shake hands. My sister Maria shared the same room with Susan almost up until the time she was married. Maria and Susan still live in the same house, and Maria, like my parents, looks after her just like she always has.

My family holds tight to an ethic of taking care of each other. We are truly each other's keepers. There was never any question of that. People ask me, "If Susan had not been disabled, how would the dynamics of the family been different?" Well, if she wasn't who she is, she wouldn't be my sister Susan. I know we are richer for having her. It has given us more insight into what life is all about. It has given us a better understanding of how everybody isn't born with the same abilities as everybody else. You have to consider yourself fortunate. Look, I grew up with a crew of tough guys, and I would cringe when I heard the word *retard*. But there are only so many battles you can fight. This sensitivity is a gift Susan has given me—given our whole family. It has made me realize that I have abilities—physical, analytical, intuitive—that other people don't have. When you see someone struggling with something, something that would be a snap for you because of your strength, size, or intellect, then help them out! Whoever has the ability to care, takes the care. I live that imperative because I learned it young. I was blessed with being in a position to help—to give strength, lend intelligence, provide defense—when I could. So I did.

That Sunday, a little after 10:00 p.m., Joy and I left Angelo's house after an episode of *The Sopranos*, a show that always left me ambivalent. In the thirty-minute drive back to Jersey City, I was already feeling the onset of my "Sunday night blues," as Joy called it. It was more like Sunday-night anxiety derived from the cold, hard fact that I had to get up insanely early for the weekly Monday morning Network Plus conference call the next day. There were fourteen Network Plus sales offices up and down the East Coast.

Where your office finished in sales for the previous week determined what time you got your call. The earliest call began at 5:00 a.m., and the latest one at 7:45 a.m. Any way you sliced it, it was an early wake-up. And Monday was all about clockwork.

MONDAY, SEPTEMBER 10, 2001

I've never been someone who, as soon as he moves into a new apartment, kicks into *Queer Eye for the Straight Guy* mode. I'm more college dormitory *anti*-chic. My basement apartment in Jersey City reflected this interior design philosophy. I'd positioned the bed in the obvious spot, slid in a couple of end tables, and made sure the TV was viewable from every angle in the apartment. I had no couch in this small space, so I watched TV from bed. It was a railroad-style apartment. First car was the living room / bedroom; then you hit the kitchen, then the bathroom. There was a door to the back patio area. My building was an old one that, to my knowledge, had never been refurbished.

I don't like getting up early. So I didn't like my 5:00 a.m. start on Mondays. I tried to make my morning rituals as unconscious as possible. I shaved. (I hate shaving. I tried to shave every other day, but it didn't really work.) I threw on a suit, I grabbed my backpack—which I used the way most people use a wallet—and I was out the door.

The advantage of taking the PATH train before rush hour was that the trains weren't crowded. The disadvantage was there weren't very many trains running. So if the PATH didn't come in on time, I was late for the Monday-morning call. Then I'd start off the day and my week in a bad mood. In my head, I would already be in a bad mood just worrying about being in a bad mood. Welcome to my Monday-morning commute.

The PATH train was, for all practical purposes, my only way to work, to the World Trade Center. I took it every day. The PATH Pavonia-Newport Station was about a half-mile walk from my apartment. It's a ten-minute ride—two stops—to the World Trade Center. I typically bought a number of tokens in advance. When I first began working at the World Trade Center office, the PATH cost $1. Now it's like two bucks and rising, but still a pretty good deal.

My daily commute had become a matter of repetition. I can still recall every step as if I'm doing it right now:

Once I go underground to catch the PATH, I never feel the outside again. Ten minutes later, the PATH doors open, and I am in the basement of the World Trade Center. I walk up a small flight of stairs and step onto a giant escalator bank, which carries me up to the main shopping area in the North Tower, or Tower 1. I walk right by the Verizon Wireless kiosk where I bought my cell phone. I walk briskly through the shopping corridor, which looks like a subset of any top mall in the country: Banana Republic, Gap, Godiva, Borders. Invariably, I stop at American Coffee and grab a cup of black with sugar. I leave the shopping area and enter the North Tower lobby. It is an enormous lobby. Off to the right is a whole row of twenty to twenty-five security desks. Turning to the left, I flash my security pass to the guard stationed behind the battery of turnstiles lined in front of the elevators. From there, I take one of several main elevators that hold up to fifty people and rocket from the lobby to the 78th floor in forty-five seconds. My ears pop every time I ride that damn elevator. I walk off the express elevator and take a "local" one to the 81st floor, which deposits me right outside the door to the Network Plus office.

We occupied the southeast corner office, seven thousand square feet with large wooden doors at the entrance. Bank of

America had just moved in across the hall. They were the only other company on the floor. If you walked a straight line to the back of our office and took a hard left, you walked into our conference room, which was located in the physical corner of the building. The view from the conference room was breathtaking. From the east window, you could see across the East River to Brooklyn with full views of the Brooklyn, Williamsburg, and Manhattan bridges. From the south window, you could see the southern tip of Manhattan Island, the Statue of Liberty, and parts of New Jersey. It felt about as New York City as any office could feel.

Kevin Nichols, the regional manager, was an early riser, and always the first in. That Monday was no exception. I grumbled as I walked by him, thinking about what I might need to address on the conference call: New sales? Big sales? New hires? New fires? What did I have in the pipeline? Was it a bad week, and why? Would I get a lambasting or a kudos? I tried to anticipate the CEO's mood. These were my big concerns.

I dropped my bag in my office, gathered some documents, and went to Kevin's office for the call. After escaping the conference call relatively unscathed, I prepared for a meeting with my entire staff at 8:15 a.m. They had to be in by 8:00 a.m. That was the rule. Whoever came in past 8:00 a.m. paid $2. If I was late, I paid $10. I got my thoughts organized about what I wanted to say to the team. I created a handout that noted the top sales of the week and included bullet points for discussion—what we had gone over during the managers' conference calls, new training, what to look for in the marketplace, product promos. I printed out forty copies.

We gathered in the conference room. I ran the meeting—delivered the information, motivated them, and prepared them to go sell for the week. I also reminded them that we needed to meet quotas and, of course, of what they needed to do to win an open bar. I always ended the meetings with some type of relevant inspirational or motivational quote. Whoever guessed the author earned a free lunch. Monday is an in day, so they hit the phones, made calls, and set up appointments. My door, I told them, was always open.

We all took the same lunch hour: 12:00 noon to 1:00 p.m. There was no flexibility with that. But man, did we treasure that hour. The courtyard of the World Trade Center was such a vibrant area. (Maybe people forget that now.) Your every want could be fulfilled in a one-to-two-block radius. The World Trade Center had its own mall with top-notch retail stores and food. If you needed a clean shirt or a new tie, Century 21 was across the street. Borders was next door. We went out to lunch as a crew. We'd grab cheap Chinese on Fulton Street or tasty Cuban from Sylvia's on Greenwich. If we didn't want to walk very far, we'd buy the tandoori chicken–basmati rice combo or something else delicious off a truck just a few yards from the North Tower's front door. Tables were set up around the courtyard's fountain. We liked eating there, outside. That time of year, that Monday, they still had bands playing near the fountain in front of the Towers.

That Monday, many of us sat in the courtyard together, drenched in the brilliant sun. I took the hour and poured myself back into *Black Hawk Down*. I found the story very engrossing, and I began to savor each page.

When I'm reading a book, I usually keep it in my trusty bag that I bring with me wherever I go. I'll read the book on the subway, on lunch break—any chance I get. This book was especially compelling to me. I loved reading about how the marines, the army, and the Delta Force all came together as a team. These men truly lived the marine code of "Leave no man behind."

There's a part in the book where the author interviewed these guys on the Delta Force, supreme human fighting machines who have chosen to make frontline combat their lives. The reason they continue to take on another tour of duty or another mission—the reason they risk their lives again and again—isn't political, financial, or because they're ordered to do so. The reason they do it is for "the guy next to you." That's what motivates them to serve.

Man, I was fortunate I never had to serve in a war. My generation didn't face any drafts. How would I react if I was placed in the most dire of circumstances, forced to fight for something important to me? Would I have the salt to perform, to do my job in the face of death or facing the fear of death? Could I overcome that fear and react?

Black Hawk Down was difficult and inspiring. It described horrible deaths and unspeakable ruthlessness, but also acts of unbelievable courage and heroic selflessness.

Two soldiers profiled in the book, Randy Shughart and Gary Gordon, were posthumously awarded the Congressional Medal of Honor. While on board a rescue Black Hawk helicopter, these soldiers saw a pilot down who was wounded, defenseless, and about to be captured by a swarm of enemy militia. They knew that even for as long as they might be able to hold off the thousand-strong enemy horde, it would not be long enough for help to arrive. Their general told them not to attempt the rescue. Yet they respectfully requested their general to allow them to go down there. The general asked them, "Do you understand what you're asking permission to do?" In other words, did they understand they had very little chance of surviving? They said they understood perfectly. Who knows what really went through their minds? Maybe they were the kind of ultimate soldiers who felt that a slim chance was chance enough. Maybe they were thrill seekers, adrenaline junkies. Maybe they saw that the fallen pilot was going to be overcome, and God knows what would have happened to him, and they reacted out of overwhelming compassion. Or maybe they just simply knew they couldn't live with themselves if they didn't do it. Only they knew. I'm sure their wives and kids would tell you they wished they hadn't done it. But they might also tell you that knowing their husbands'/ fathers' codes as human beings and soldiers the way they did, it was the only course of action the men could take. I don't think I've ever had a more palpable emotional moment reading a book than I did reading that part of *Black Hawk Down.*

By the end of Monday, most of the office was talking about the Giants playing *Monday Night Football.* A lot of guys planned to see the game out somewhere in the city. I left the office around 6:30 p.m. and made plans to watch the game at home with Joy. The Giants lost in Denver 31–20. Late in the fourth quarter, I called my old friend Boozer to complain about the Giants' ineptitude. He told me something about it being "a long season." I was not consoled.

It was almost 1:00 a.m. Joy had been asleep since the third quarter. It was harder, in a way, to wake up for Tuesdays than for Mondays. By Tuesday the full workweek had set in. The buzz of the weekend was over, and the next weekend seemed as far away as it could be. I didn't know what this particular Tuesday would bring, but I knew it would feel like the longest day of the week.

PART II

THE DAY

TUESDAY, SEPTEMBER 11, 2001

Despite staying up late watching the Giants game, I planned to go in early on Tuesday. It was an out day. I had to get people out to their appointments.

In order to get to work by 7:30 a.m., I had to make it to the PATH by 7:15 a.m. Joy didn't need to be at Atlantic Records on the Upper West Side until 10:00 a.m., but she got up with me and drove me to the PATH. She dropped me off at the station with a quick kiss good-bye. Joy says there was something different about the way we said good-bye that morning. She remembers not saying "Have a great day." (Joy often kidded me about how the voice mail messages on my cell phone and office phone ended with a semi-tough, semi-sincere "Have a great day.") She regrets not saying more that morning. We were both in good moods, as I recall. What I distinctly remember—and it strikes me about as ironic as anything ever will—was that on 1010 WINS radio that morning, they were talking about how Mayor Giuliani was declaring that day as 911 Awareness Day in New York in order to promote citizens properly utilizing 911. I don't know if they still have 911 Awareness Day. I don't think so.

On the PATH ride in, I finished the last pages of *Black Hawk Down*. The book filled me with so many feelings. A lot of people got killed. There was savagery on both sides. But all in all, this group of guys kept together. At its core, it's a story of survival—getting out of this nasty situation, a human hornet's nest—by sticking together. One thing that really struck me was how the men reacted when a simple in-and-out forty-five-minute mission went horribly wrong, and, when things continued to go wrong, how they kept overcoming obstacles despite facing the very real threat of death. What they endured in those twelve hours went beyond remarkable. I made a mental note to return the book to Mike Wright, from whom I borrowed it, once I got back to the office.

I got to work earlier than usual. Looking out our conference room window, admiring the magnificent vista, I could see it was already a beautiful day—blue skies, no clouds, orange sunshine.

There was only one other person in the office: Kevin Nichols. *Did the guy sleep there?* I parked myself at the reception desk, to have a good look at my sales reps as they rolled in. I sat there from 7:50 a.m. to 8:20 a.m. Marc Reinstein got to work on time. He and I talked about the Giants game while several of us did the *Daily News* crossword puzzle. Kevin boasted that he was almost done with his. I went into my office and gazed south out my window, overlooking the lower tip of Manhattan. Man, was it ever a picture-postcard day.

I called Gina Menella in to "remind" her that she was late again. She wasn't happy with me reminding her about it and collecting the $2. She left in a huff. I checked my Day-Timer to see what appointments I had scheduled. I began drafting a list, pairing newer hires with veterans. I grew concerned that some of our salespeople were still in the office when it was already well past 8:00 a.m., as it took a half hour to get to a Midtown appointment from the World Trade Center. I kept that concern to myself, for the moment. I paired Marc Reinstein with Jen Sotack and assigned them to the Diamond District. Who next?

All of a sudden, it felt like a hectic morning. My mind was racing. I wanted to keep people moving and to make sure they got to their appointments on time. I wanted to confirm that the right people were going to the right appointments, see that everyone going out was properly prepared and provided coverage for any incoming deals. And then it hit me like a ton of bricks as it did several times that summer: *I'm working my ass off while the stock is in the tank. I lost all my dough. I am engaged to be married. I have to pay for a wedding.* But hey, on that particular morning, I wasn't late to work. I had time to joke with people. The weather looked good, so I felt good. It was an out day. That's what I lived for. To get out there in the city and walk the streets, ride the subway, and be in front of people. Sure, I had the wedding on my mind. I knew how much it would cost. I knew I had a down payment to make. I knew I couldn't rely on my stock options because the stock was in the tank. I didn't know when or if I'd ever be able to cash them in. Nobody knew if the stock would ever rebound. All I knew was I had to make my monthly nut. And the way I did that was by selling, running the sales force, and keeping myself motivated. I thought now, more than ever, I had reason to do that. *Try to simplify life: Save for your wedding and honeymoon.*

It was September 11. Summer was over. Labor Day was two weekends ago. It was time to start cranking. Extended vacations were over, and people were back in work mode. Companies were thinking about how to improve their bottom lines and how to streamline their operations. Telecommunications had a lot to do with that. So we had to be ready to hustle. We needed to hit the ground running. Better numbers were expected from us now that it was fall. Technically, this was the first real out day of the second half of our fiscal year, and I was ready for it.

8:30 a.m.

I brought Marc Reinstein and Jen Sotack in to my office. She had been with the company only six months and was having some trouble selling. I saw potential in Jen, and I wanted Marc to go out with her on an appointment. It was a good appointment, and I knew Marc could help her. I looked at Marc and remembered hiring him a year and a half earlier. He was iffy then. Through sheer hustle, the young guy had developed into an excellent salesman. I was proud of him.

I sent Marc and Jen on their way, sat down at my desk, and called my buddy Paul Rubicam. Ruby worked for a big real estate firm down in Philadelphia. I met him years ago through my college roommate at Brown, while Ruby was playing soccer at Penn, where his father was athletic director. When I first started with Network Plus, Ruby and I lived together down in Princeton. He is the only post-college roommate I've ever had. I buzzed him to see what he was up to and to bust his chops. He picks up the phone and answers, with a big sigh, "What do you want, Harry?" No hello. Typical Ruby.

"What kind of a greeting is that?" I said.

"Listen, you're costing me money. I got some high-powered attorney in my office who is charging me—how much are you charging me?" I don't hear any response. "You just cost me $500."

"All right, Ruby, I'll talk to you later." I hung up the phone.

8:46 a.m.

I peeked out my office doorway and saw Marc Reinstein messing with some papers.

"Reinstein, why aren't you out the door?"

That was the last moment of normalcy—seeing Marc Reinstein. That's when it happened.

First I heard Jim Gaffney scream, like I'd never heard a man scream, "OH MY GOD!" I'll never forget that scream.

In our office, Jim was standing closest to the impact. My corner office was located all the way on the south side of the building. You couldn't get any farther south in the building than I was. The plane hit the north side. If you walked directly north from my corner office, you would go straight through the huge wooden doors at the office's entrance, which stood in front of two banks of three elevators. That was the northernmost point of our office. Before you passed through those wooden doors, there was a little wall mirror, which salespeople liked to use to "button up" before leaving for an appointment. Jim Gaffney was in front of that mirror checking his tie when the plane hit. The impact blew in those huge wooden office doors, coming within inches of striking Jim.

I heard Jim screaming, and a second later, I felt the impact. I felt it more than I heard it. It wasn't a sharp *boom* or *pow* like a gunshot, but a deep, expansive sound. It was less of a sound and more of a vibration—a percussive rumble that sounded *and* felt like it was closing in on you.

Sitting in the southernmost point of the office, I was the last to feel it. I stood up slowly. God knows why, but I was strangely calm. It didn't register with me that we were in the midst of a terrible, profound emergency. I remember thinking, *OK, this is something bad,* but another part of my brain immediately disciplined me. *It's nothing. Whatever it is, be calm. Deal with it. Figure it out.* But the screams from people out in the office conveyed another message entirely. To hear sounds like those from grown men and women—sounds of sheer terror—and to see looks of paralyzing uncertainty—it shocked me as much for its bizarre nature as for its stark reality. My reaction to their screams was just as odd. I reacted with a half-annoyed "What the hell is going on out there? You people should be working!" attitude and half "I'm not sure what the hell's really happening right now because they are really acting weird out there." A big part of me felt that I had to assume my head-of-the-office role.

I yelled at everyone: "Calm down. What the hell is going on! Calm down now!" I swung around and looked out my office window behind me. I saw bright orange flames shooting out and down from directly above me. I didn't know it at the time, but what I saw was the nose of the airliner pushing through the tower's south end. It didn't go through, but it pushed in enough that fire exploded out through broken windows. Chunks of the building and paper debris burst in the air, creating what I can only describe as a large, dirty cloud.

Looking back now, I'm amazed that I wasn't more alarmed. It was pretty intense, horror film stuff. I say this not to impress anybody; it's just that to this day, I'm surprised at my own reaction. I've had some time to think about why I wasn't terrified and overcome with fear from the obviously deadly catastrophe that I was looking at right outside my window. It could be that because we're so used to seeing this kind of thing on TV and film on a daily basis, it didn't look like anything that catastrophic. It's funny how faulty perception can work to your advantage in a situation like this. Even though you felt the impact and you felt the building shaking—and all of that felt catastrophic—you never think *you* are in real danger. You don't know what real danger is, because you've never been in it. That ignorance may have been the only thing that kept me from lapsing into petrified terror. In my head, I was thinking, *Well, real danger is something much, much greater than this. I'm still standing. It didn't knock me off my feet. How bad could it be?* These are the games you play in your head to internalize a sense of relative safety, to give yourself a chance to avoid thinking the unthinkable. I did that immediately. It was no conscious act of bravery, just an unconscious reflex. Or maybe it was a subconscious choice, or just luck—a random confluence of factors, added up from my entire life, leading me up to this critical cognitive moment. For whatever reason, I stepped to the right, mentally, when I could've stepped to the left. I'll never know for sure, but that mental dodge may have made all the difference. That's what you do when you have no idea what's really going on.

Marc Reinstein completely froze. He thought the building was going to fall over because that's how much the tower was swaying. *Holy shit, the World Trade Center is swaying!* I noticed it too. This swaying was not merely perceptible. It was palpable. I can explain the difference. Standing at the urinal in the men's room on the 81st floor, one could, guided by the bellwether compass of one's discharge, observe the clear sway of the building. You could only really notice it in the men's room. I never felt it in my office. But we always knew the tower swayed. This wasn't like that. This was more like *leaning*, not swaying.

Time to Get Out

I quickly came to accept that there was something serious going on above us. But there was no reason for panic. Some reps were diving under cubicles. Some lost control of their legs. They didn't know whether to stand or fall or what. Women were screaming. Guys were hugging other guys. Everyone was grabbing on to someone. (Marc Reinstein remained frozen.) And all I'm doing is yelling, "Calm down. Calm down."

I needed to act. The first thing I did was assess the damage. Flames were coming from the south. The big wooden doors that were always locked were blown open from the north. I ran through the office, outside the blown-open doors, and looked in the hallway at the elevators. The Sheetrock walls around the elevator banks were bending inward. The elevators would be of no use. I looked left toward the bathroom, but ceiling tiles and large pieces of the walls lay scattered and broken on the floor in the hallway, impeding access to the entrance. I looked to the right. The staircase was clear. Nothing obstructed it. I turned around, facing north, and noticed more debris. Then I saw someone emerge from the office across the hall on the north side of the floor, staggering and bloodied. I'd seen enough.

I ran back into my office. People were maintaining relative calm. Somebody shouted that there were people stuck in the bathroom. I yelled back, "I'll take care of it." I made a mental note, but first things first. I knew for sure that the flames were to the south and that something bad was going on to the north. So I yelled in no uncertain terms, "Everyone: Move to the center of the office." I wanted them all in one place, together. Everyone moved. Kevin Nichols held tight to our receptionist, who was crying. Mike Wright came toward me and said, "Ben,"—that's what they called me at work sometimes, short for *Benfante*— "we've got to get everyone out of here." Yes, that was the next step. I knew the stairwell was clear. So I sent the group to the stairwell exit. We moved quickly, decisively, and intelligently. Nobody left anybody behind. These were good people. They exited in clusters of two or three—always one with another— nobody alone. They looked out for each other. It was not a spirit of every man for himself. I heard them tell of more of this type of behavior in their stories later on. I credit the amazing fact that they all made it out safely in the end to their collective sense of responsibility to each other. I couldn't have been more proud of these people, many of whom I had hired and some of whom I'd known for years.

I was reminded that people were stuck in the bathroom. I darted back into the elevator hallway, climbed over knee-high piles of broken ceiling tile and chunks of Sheetrock, and finally got down to the men's room. More people started to emerge from the office across the hall on the north side. So many had blood all over their faces. My sense of urgency heightened, I shifted into "moving mode." As long as I was moving, I was fine. That would be the basic guiding principle from that moment until the end of the experience: *Keep moving and you'll be OK—at least you'll feel like you'll be OK. Don't stop moving.*

I punched in the touch key combination to the men's room, opened the door—and there was nobody in sight. Good thing. The place was demolished. The stalls were collapsed. Water was spraying everywhere. Smoke filled the room, making it hard to see. It looked as though a bomb had gone off. I wasn't going farther in than I had to. I yelled, "Anybody in there?" No response. Later, I found out that they wanted me to help the people stuck in the women's bathroom, not the men's. I heard that some other guys eventually kicked down that women's room door, which had become stuck, and everybody got out safely.

I left the men's room, climbed back over the debris, returned to the office, and saw that people were filing down the stairs in an orderly fashion. I ran all the way into my office, grabbed my cell phone and my trusty bag. I strapped it across my chest, and as I turned to leave, I spotted the copy of *Black Hawk Down* on my desk. I hesitated. I had meant to return it to Mike Wright that morning. *I'll give it to him when we come back up later.* Dashing out, I was startled to notice that the windows on the east side of the whole office were badly shattered; shards of broken glass were scattered all over the desks a few feet away. Joe Longorino and Phil Ipsan, the reps who sat there, were already out on appointments. I used to sit there when I first came to the office.

I checked the perimeter offices to make sure they were really all clear. Adam Andrews, the assistant manager, waited with me and helped make sure everyone was gone. There were no fire alarms or sprinklers going off. What else was there to do? Adam and I headed to the stairwell. I was the last man out. Only three or four minutes had passed since impact.

Heading Down the Stairs

There were not a lot of people in the stairwell, at first. There were mostly those from my floor and some injured people scrambling. The injuries varied—some bleeding, some burned, some applying makeshift bandages to their wounds. Some of the uninjured walked cautiously, like old people walking on an icy sidewalk. Others gave aid to the injured. All were moving. Some quicker than others, but moving. The prevailing attitude was generally calm.

Off the stairwell, on the 79th floor, we heard two guys yelling for help behind elevator doors. We managed to open them enough to see that the elevator car was stuck in between the 80th and 79th floors. I ran into a nearby office and grabbed one of those bathroom keys that have a stick attached so no one walks off with it. Another guy used the leg of a metal chair. Prying the doors open, it looked like we would kink them, doing more damage than good. We realized our effort was futile. We opened up the doors just enough to shove the stick attached to the key and left it with them. We said good luck and kept moving. This all happened very fast. It took less than a minute.

I got back into the stairwell and regained my spot behind Adam Andrews again. I was moving. On the 79th floor, my phone rang. According to my cell phone records, I got the call at 8:52 a.m. It was Joy. She was frantic. "Oh my god, where are you? Michael, what's going on?"

"I'm fine," I told her. "I'm in the stairwell. I'm heading down, and I'm OK."

I thought I was having this conversation with her. I thought I was allaying her fears. But the line was breaking up on her end, so I finally assured her, "Look, I'm fine, really. I'll call you when I get to the bottom." I hung up. I came to find out later that she never heard a word I said. I could hear her, but all she could hear was static. In my mind, I thought I had talked to my fiancée and she knew I was OK. She was having another experience entirely. What she went through as events unfolded was an emotional hell ride that so many loved ones endured that day. For so many, that tortured experience of waiting and not knowing had a very different conclusion. That I made it out and others didn't still haunts me terribly.

We proceeded to the 78th floor, where the express elevator stopped. People moved quickly and efficiently down the stairs. It wasn't crowded. I began to wonder what the hell was really happening. I heard people screaming. I kept getting different versions of what was going on. One person said definitely, "There's a fire!" I saw a fire extinguisher out of the safety glass sitting on the stairwell landing on the 76th floor, so I grabbed it and began to head back up the stairs.

It was simple to me: People were yelling "There's a fire!" I was standing next to a fire extinguisher, and nobody was using it. I figured, *Why don't we do something?*

I started to go back up, but I wasn't getting anywhere. Too many people were on the stairwell heading in the opposite direction. I got up maybe a flight and a half. *This is crazy.* I put the fire extinguisher down and resumed my descent.

Not even two steps back down the stairwell, I ran into John Cerqueira. I had hired John three months earlier right out of college. Here was a guy who was classic sales material—six feet tall, all-American good looks, well-spoken. He looked nervous. I wondered what he was doing by himself. I didn't remember seeing him in the office when all hell had broken loose. He was stuck in the bathroom when the explosion hit. Then he moved to a mechanical room, where he and some other people were stuck for a while. Now both of us were well behind the others in our office.

"Let's stick together on the way down," I said. That made good sense to both of us.

We hurried down the stairs. Things moved well at this point. Some people had minor cuts and scrapes, but nobody was hurt badly enough to stop the flow of human traffic. There was no panic. It felt like we were moving, so I felt OK. I didn't feel I was in danger.

There was some talk in the stairwell that it was a plane that hit the building. I imagined a small commuter plane went off course. No big deal.

But the stories and theories kept on flying. Some sounded plausible, and some sounded outrageous. I didn't say much. I took it all in. The wheels in my mind were turning in multiple directions. Sure, I wanted to know what the actual problem was, but mostly I thought, *Let's get out of here first.* I actually could've moved even faster down the stairs. I wasn't impaired physically in any way like some were. But I wanted to stay with John, and I didn't want to be rude and just blow by everyone in an every-man-for-himself kind of way. We here heading down the stairs at a good pace. That was fine with me.

The 68th Floor

The network of stairwells and landings were well lit, one indistinguishable from the next. The small victories were seeing the floor numbers go down floor by floor. At each landing we could see the floor entrances. Sometimes the entrance doors were open, and sometimes they weren't. On the 68th floor, they were wide open. I observed someone there calmly walk into the stairwell, then back into the office floor. That was odd.

I walked out of the stairwell and onto the 68th floor. I thought I should tell the others, "Hey, the stairwell is pretty clear. C'mon, let's go." I also wanted to see if I could find out what was going on. Maybe I could see something from there.

John followed me. We said we would stick together.

There was a badly damaged Snapple vending machine in the office lobby. The glass casing showed what looked like a man-made smash in the middle of it. You could just grab a Snapple.

I told whomever I passed that the stairway was all clear. Some of them began to head toward it. I turned right down one hallway, which opened up into another long hallway on the right. At the end of the hallway, there were large see-through glass doors that were the threshold to more office space. Three women stood huddled on the other side of the doors. They were just standing there, together, still. Maybe they didn't know?

I ran down the hallway leading toward the glass doors. I banged on the glass. They hit the Open button, and before I could open my mouth to tell them anything, one of them stepped aside, revealing a fourth woman sitting in a motorized wheelchair.

She wasn't a very big person. She was quite small, in fact. "Is she OK?" I asked. They didn't answer but instead solemnly looked down at their friend in the wheelchair.

The woman in the wheelchair stared straight ahead at no one in particular. I looked at her straight in the face.

"Do you need help?"

"Yes," she said. No hesitation.

It was strange to me. Here were these women standing together. There were no men. It appeared as though everyone had already cleared out of the office. And when I asked her "Do you need help?" I sincerely meant it. It was as if maybe she was waiting for somebody, some formal procedure or the firemen. So when I asked her this question, I didn't have a specific plan of action in mind about how I would help her or what help I could offer. It was more of a general question that could've elicited a number of responses.

But she said one word: "Yes."

The woman was calm. Her face showed noticeable concern, but she was in control. Her diminutive frame belied a definite strength she communicated through her clear and serious blue eyes. This was not a person who perceived herself as helpless in the world. Though I would later learn that her hands were clenched from rheumatoid arthritis since the age of three and her build was ever so slight, she projected a presence that indicated more ability than disability.

I wondered how long she might have been waiting there. The three women held her personal belongings. I sensed they were her friends.

An evacuation chair lay flat on the floor next to her. It looked like a folded beach chair attached to a lightweight hand truck with wheels and sliders on the bottom. It was all folded up with Velcro straps.

Keep moving, my inner voice told me. A thousand thoughts flooded my brain. My mind was racing. She needed help. What was the next move? Whatever it was, the voice in my head was unequivocal: *Move!*

I tried to open the evac chair. I fiddled with the straps, but the straps weren't what kept the chair from opening. In my head I was screaming: *How do you open this fucking thing!* Finally, I saw this little lever on the bottom. I hit the lever. The chair opened. The Velcro straps were there for the purpose of strapping the person in the wheelchair, not strapping the wheelchair together. Now I know.

We placed the woman in the evac chair. She repeatedly expressed concern about leaving her motorized wheelchair behind. They're very costly. John went to get it.

"Leave it, John," I said. "It's too cumbersome. It's way too heavy. We'll come back up later and get it for her."

I could see the woman didn't like my plan. I bent down, looked her in the eye, and assured her, "Look, we can't get you out of here and carry that wheelchair too. I promise you, I will personally come back up here and get that wheelchair for you."

She nodded in agreement. She was a decisive person. That was good. John still insisted. "We can take it, Mike. Really, we can."

I looked at him, perhaps unconsciously prevailing upon our boss-employee relationship. "Leave it and grab a side of this evac chair."

Carrying her, not wheeling her, made the most sense. It was faster, plain and simple. Plus, it let us move at the pace our feet would carry us. Was she heavy? Well, she wasn't light, but the real challenge was balance. Keeping her level while moving down the stairs was our main concern. If we didn't distribute the weight evenly, she could tip over. John took one side of the evac chair, and I took the other, which made us a three-person load coming down the right side of the stairs. As long as we concentrated, I felt that we could make it.

"Here we go," I said to the woman.

"One second," she said, putting on a surgical mask. "OK. Let's go."

We carried her. Her friends carried her belongings. And we headed into the stairwell, hoping to get out as quickly as possible.

Floors 68–55

John and I carried her from the 68th to the 55th floor. My prime directive was still *Keep moving*. Anytime there was a little stoppage or the stairwell got crowded, I tried to figure out our next move. I was always looking ahead, thinking ahead. With each step my role as navigator became more and more defined.

What little talking we did, John did most of it with the woman in the wheelchair. I was figuring out how to get around people and making sure there wasn't anyone or anything in our way. I simply wanted to keep us moving forward.

This wasn't a chitchat atmosphere. We were tense. Our limited dialogue consisted of the frequent "You OK? You all right?" from me and nods of assent from her. *Keep moving.*

We rapidly made our way to the 55th floor, where somehow someone had created an impromptu water station. Many were leaving the stairwell to rehydrate. It made sense to us to stop there too. John and I set the woman down on the office's foyer floor. Then John went to grab himself some water in one of the adjacent offices. I asked the woman if she wanted some water. She moved her surgical mask to the side to answer: No. "Are you sure?"

"No," she said.

Why wouldn't she want water? "Well, I'm setting you down here for a moment, and I'm getting some water." I looked at her through the mask. "I'll be right back." But she didn't look right to me. *Did she say she didn't want water because she didn't want me to leave her? Did she think I was leaving her?* I sensed she wasn't telling me all she really felt. I turned back around. "Don't go anywhere." I wasn't being facetious. I meant to assure her I was coming back. Her changeless mixed expression of calm and concern remained as earnest as it was when I first saw her. I didn't know what to make of it. I took one last look at her and walked toward an office.

The truth is I didn't want water. I wanted to see what was going on. I thought maybe people on this floor might know something. And I knew I had to be quick.

I ran toward a window in an office space and looked out eastward over the courtyard. I saw all forms of detritus strewn about on the ground far below, but it was hard to make out exactly what it was. For a split second, I thought that some of the things I saw on the ground were bodies. As quickly as that thought entered my mind, another part of my brain immediately shut it down. How could I be sure? We were so high up. But at that point, it mentally and emotionally registered to me that something was very, very wrong. Danger was near, maybe closer than I realized.

I ran from the window to a desk with a phone. I called my parents' house. I dialed but couldn't get through. I dialed again and still couldn't get through. I dialed a third time and got my father.

"Dad!"

"Jesus Christ, Michael! What's going on? Where are you? Are you OK?"

"I'm fine. I'm helping a woman in a wheelchair."

"You have to get out of there, *now*."

"I'm getting out. I might try to look for an elevator to go down."

He thought I said I was *in* an elevator. He was so excited that he didn't hear a lot of what I was saying.

"Dad, I'm all right. I'll call you as soon as I get out."

My father had already seen it all on TV. He saw the plane hit my building, just twelve floors above my office. He saw the second plane hit the South Tower. He knew the gravity of the situation, but I didn't give him enough time to tell me. I wanted to keep moving.

I hung up on my father. I hustled back to the woman in the wheelchair. I brought her water. She drank it.

I got the vague sense from my father's voice that something more serious than I thought was taking place. But as serious as I imagined it might be, I thought that at worst he was telling me to get out of a building that had a fire in it, *somewhere.* I thought the fire was high above me, and that I was out of danger. But my father knew how bad my situation was. Worse, in his mind, he was thinking I was in an elevator, which is a very bad place to be in a building fire. On top of that, I'd told him I was helping a woman in a wheelchair, so he knew I wasn't moving as fast as I could.

It was, in fact, at 9:02 a.m., sometime between when we began carrying the woman in the wheelchair and the 55th floor, that the second plane hit the South Tower. The stairwells were very well insulated. You couldn't hear a lot. We heard none of it. In a matter of minutes, within those thirteen floors, our grave danger had doubled in scope, and we knew nothing of it.

John and I picked the woman back up and resumed our descent. Though it had only been thirteen floors, we had effectively established our carrying positions: me on the left navigating, John on the right.

From floor to floor, men jumped in intermittently to help us. There were handles on the front of the wheelchair. That made it easier. When offers to help came forth, John and I took the front handles, and various men took turns holding the back. Some stayed longer than others. But eventually each left to move faster. We were moving. That was all I cared about. But what if we stopped moving? Then what?

Floors 55–33: We See Firemen

Two things became more evident the lower we descended down the stairs: We moved slower, and we saw firemen.

Things got really backed up. The firemen told us to stay to the right so they could make their way up the left side of the stairwell. That slowed the flow of traffic considerably. It also made two men carrying a woman in a wheelchair a very inconvenient way to travel down the stairs. Turning a corner was always a negotiation for us. Because we were three across, the firemen had to make an exception for us. They let us pass on the left or go to our right, whichever worked better.

You could hear broken-voiced dispatches coming through the firemen's radio devices, which made people in the stairwell think they had information we didn't. People hectored them with questions, trying to find out what was going on. For our own protection, they never gave a complete or straight answer. That kept me calm. It didn't allow me to dwell too much on what could really be going on, or if and to what degree our lives were in danger. What good would it do for us to know what happened? Would it move us down the stairs faster? It might set off panic. Could they have even described the entire situation if they tried? Lack of information kept me concentrated on moving forward.

To this day, I can't get those firemen out of my mind. I see their faces. With each one I passed, I saw in their eyes extreme exhaustion and extreme determination. Those looks shot right through me then, and they still do now. I must have seen fifty, maybe a hundred—sweating, lugging heavy gear, knowing what we didn't know, knowing they were headed toward incredible personal danger, risking their lives to help others. But despite their load, their fatigue, and their rush into danger, they calmed all of us. They told us in reassuring tones, "Just keep going." They were professional. Through their manner and movement, they spoke to us without speaking: *You'll make it.* Never once did they let us know how dire the situation was. "Keep moving. It's gonna be OK," they'd say. They were very positive, very steady. They gave us what we needed. And we kept moving.

The more I think back on their faces, the more I realize that they didn't simply look tired. Their expression said more than

This is unbelievably hard. Will I make it up all these stairs? It went beyond that. It was more of an expression of profound knowing. It said, *I know the gravity of what's going on around me here.* They knew it was an incomprehensibly bad situation. They knew we had been attacked. They knew what airplane fuel could do. Of course, this was a physically challenging rescue that went beyond the wildest imaginable and most brutal training manual scenario. Sure they were tired. But they were more pensive than tired. These firemen understood that in this matter of life and death, they were doubtless heading toward the latter. And they walked into it with such bravery, dignity, and stoicism.

Of the handful of instances I remember of civilians selflessly helping firemen, I'll never forget one man, stripped down to his T-shirt and suit pants, who, seeming like he might be a volunteer fireman in his hometown, moved quickly past me carrying a heavy fire hose. He was an Asian-American man who looked to be in good shape. He appeared very much like a man on a mission who knew what he was doing. The firemen told him, "It's OK, you can set it down." And the man said, "No, it's all right. I can handle it. I feel good." The firemen kept saying "Don't worry about it," and the guy continued to insist he could help.

I should do more than I'm doing now. I'm just carrying this woman down. Anyone can do this. Maybe I should trade off with somebody in the stairwell and go help the firemen. That Asian man is helping. How incredibly noble! The firemen look tired. They've got to carry up more stuff than I'm carrying. Why don't I help them? I paused for just a moment. John and the woman looked at me quizzically. The firemen were still telling the Asian man to set the hose down. *If I let go of the evac chair, it will just be another fireman that takes her down, and he'll be taken away from saving another life.* It's amazing how your mind rushes to calculate risk-benefit in a situation like that. It does this in fractions of a second. I stared into the eyes of the woman in the wheelchair, and then looked straight ahead. I reminded myself of what I was doing. *Keep moving. Get us out.* I would learn what those firemen knew soon enough.

Floors 33–21: Getting Lower, Moving Slower

The farther down we went, the longer it took to get from floor to floor. Conditions worsened. The human traffic had increased twofold in number. The exodus had become increasingly diverse. Some women carried their shoes, others went shoeless. There were bandaged people, bloodied people, people wearing far less of the clothing they wore to work that morning. Everyone was sweating. And always, always firemen. Heavyset people leaned on banisters for a moment, for a few moments, breathing heavily, regrouping themselves in order to go on. Older people wheezed and sat down to rest, if only to catch their breath. For many it was just a simple matter of fatigue anyone would experience traveling the sheer number of floors. We counted floors like you count repetitions in gym workout: down the stairs, hit a level, hit floor. Repeat. When would this be over? The monotony was compounded by the steady rise in temperature. The air became thicker with more people sharing the limited oxygen in the stairwell. It was hot. It was uncomfortable. After the 33rd floor, it became a challenge to keep moving at any pace.

I *had* to keep moving.

If I was moving, I felt OK. My survival instinct was placated. Any pause, any halt in our progress alarmed me. Standing around made me very, very nervous. If we weren't moving, my mind shifted away from hopeful thinking about the next move to fearful thinking about why we were stopped. Were the exits

blocked? Did someone else need help? Any restriction of movement compromised my sense of invincibility and control, the
belief that I could get out of a situation because of my speed or
my strength. That was the way I'd always viewed myself. If you
trap me, take away my ability to move, then who am I? I wasn't
trapped helping this woman. I was merely slowed. As long as I
was moving, I was still in control of my situation. When I wasn't
moving, I was not in control; I was being controlled. That's
when I started to hear the tiny distress signal in the back of my
head. And that's precisely the signal I was trying to mute.

Sometimes the stoppage was due to having to let firemen
go up the stairs. That was better than being stopped and not
knowing why. Whatever the case was, the slow pace, the slow
descent heightened tension among the people on the stairs.

As I looked around, it became clear to me that everyone on
the stairwell was in a state of semi-shock. Nobody was talking to
each other in a normal way. We were a zombie-like procession
of tired, blank faces occasionally mustering up enough strength
to show fear and to take the next physical step forward. The
challenge was to do anything to keep oneself in reality, in the
present, and out of shock. As we moved from floor to floor, I'd
see somebody crying or bloodied. I'd ask them, "Are you OK?"
They'd say, "Yes," "No," "I think so." Then we'd keep moving.
Offering to comfort another was one of the best ways to feel
some power and control in what was a helpless situation. Little
gestures like that, no matter how ineffectual, reminded you of
your humanity. Those little gestures kept me grounded in reality,
kept me sane, and kept me moving forward.

For John, me, and the woman in the wheelchair, little had
changed. It was me on the left and John on the right, constantly
reminding each other to keep her balanced. Adrenaline overrode
fatigue.

At the 31st-floor landing, the doors to the office floor were open. As I carried the woman in the wheelchair around another corner, I glanced over my shoulder and saw a fireman on his back. His chest was heaving. He was choking. He was having a heart attack. A man tried to help him. It looked pretty bad. I looked at John, and he looked at me. I nodded to the next step in front of us. We kept moving.

On the 28th floor, I reported to the next fireman I saw. "Listen," I said. "There's a fireman a few floors up who looks like he's having a heart attack."

"I know," the fireman said. Pensive resignation was written all over his face, indicating that he'd just gotten a call on his radio. He stared down at John and me carrying the woman and spoke to me at close range. "You could set her down on the 21st floor. There's a medic station set up there, and they can take care of her."

I looked back at the woman. "Do you want us to set you down on the 21st floor?" She looked back, didn't speak, but communicated instead with a slight shrug, which I took to mean *Whatever you think is best.*

I needed her to tell me what she really wanted. But before I could open my mouth to ask her, the human log jam suddenly cleared. As if on reflex, the three of us moved as quickly as possible, moving toward the 21st floor as fast as we had done with the previous floors. I turned to the woman again. "Listen, would you like us to set you down here?" She equivocated. Did she think that I wanted to set her down? I didn't want to do it. I only said it because the fireman said it. Here we were on the 21st floor, and I wanted her to know that if she wanted to stay there for medical attention, it was entirely her call.

I thought back to when I first found her on the 68th floor. Those women were standing around her, and I'd asked, "Does she need help?" Her friends didn't answer. When I looked at the woman straight in the face and asked her "Do you need help?" she said "Yes," and I could tell she meant it.

I looked at her like I did that first time.

"Look, I'll take you all the way out of here if you want me to. Just tell me what you want me to do."

"Don't let go," she said. "I want to stay with you."

I have since learned that the woman I was carrying was someone who worked very hard for her independence. I doubt she felt comfortable asking *anyone* straight up for help, and a complete stranger, no less. I'm sure in any other circumstance she would have said to me, "If you want to set me down here, then yes, set me down." But this was a situation where she needed my help, and there was no way, from the moment I saw her, that I was not going to help. She would not let go. I would not set her down. We had come too far. Little did we know that the longest part of our journey together was ahead of us.

Floors 21–5: Time Is Running Out

On the 21st floor, movement in the stairwell slowed down to the point where we no longer measured progress by floors. We measured it by whether we advanced a step. The atmosphere changed dramatically. People were on edge. Everybody was operating on their own theory of what was really happening. Uncertainty led to more fear, and the fear fueled greater uncertainty. The physical and emotional strain was starting to show. Desperation germinated all around us. We felt it. The scenery changed as well. On these lower floors we saw more and more injured people. They were everywhere. Whoever had gotten this far had paid a visible price. Cuts and torn clothing. Heads wrapped in bandages. All around darkened hallways. Cracks in walls, water seeping through. It truly looked like a horror movie. But this was real.

On the 10th floor, we were greeted by a tremendous rumbling sound. Powerful vibrations shook the floors under our feet and the railings under our hands, yet we could see nothing. John and I looked at each other wide-eyed, sharing the same thought without speaking it: What in God's name was *that*? We both looked down at the woman. She stared straight ahead. We looked back at each other and shook our heads as if to say, *What next?* I nodded to John, indicating, *Let's keep going.* We knew something significant was happening because the entrance doors at the 10th-floor landing were different than the entrance doors at every previous landing. At every other floor, if you wanted to leave the stairwell and enter a floor, you had to pull the heavy entrance doors open toward you. But at the 10th-floor landing, a breeze came through with such force that the office doors blew open. The open doors blocked our three-person chain from getting through the landing to the next set of stairs. I had to hold the wheelchair in one hand and, with all my might, push the door closed with my other arm and hold it closed until we got completely clear of the landing. Once I let go, the door violently swung open again. Even without carrying a woman in a wheelchair, many people couldn't handle the doors on the 10th floor.

We didn't know it, and we couldn't see it, but that massive rumbling was the South Tower falling. All reports have this occurring at 9:59 a.m. John, the woman, and I had been inseparable for almost an hour.

And then, on the 7th floor, things stopped. I gripped my side of the wheelchair tightly, perhaps for the first time feeling the burden of its weight. We stood there, anxious and still, at the top of the stairwell that connected the 7th floor to the 6th. I could see all the way to the bottom of the stairwell. No one was moving. *Should we get off the stairs and find another way?*

I could no longer waste any time trying to figure out what the exact nature of the danger was. All my figuring had to be about getting us out of there. That was it. And the closer we got to getting out—the 7th floor was pretty close—the more I desperately wanted out. I knew at that moment that things were taking too long. We had to find a way out, fast. I knew whatever it was that was causing the holdup had to be bad, and that time was running out.

I was not alone in feeling intense pressure to get out. The feeling among the halted train of people became less of common community and more like that of a caravan of disparate, disgruntled refugees. Faces darkened. Hopes dimmed. Kindness dissipated. A heavyset man moved slowly through the 6th-floor doorway, and some in the crowd let slip moans of impatience. Tension in the stairwell reached its breaking point. Fear began to manifest itself in different ways. Mine was a quiet fear. Others vocalized their desperation. The louder people got, the quieter I became. The more they panicked, the more I focused. Finally, the bubble burst. I stood there dead quiet in that dark stairwell, while everyone around me was yelling, "We've got to move! What's holding it up! My god, we have to get out of here!"

In his play *No Exit*, Jean-Paul Sartre famously penned the line "Hell is other people." Where the hell was our exit?

The 5th Floor

On the 5th floor we came to a dead stop. There was no movement at all. We had come to a crossroads. John, the woman, and I left the stairwell and went out onto the floor. We had to. It was a good decision if for no other reason than the fact that we were moving again. Some people chose to stay in the stairwell. Before we got to this point, all common sense said to stay with the crowd, which was moving, even if slowly at times, toward the bottom. That was no longer the case. It was no longer clear that it was safer to stay on the stairs. Nothing was obvious now. At this point, no one felt that one direction would definitely get you out. It wasn't quite every man for himself, but you felt free to find your own way out.

On the 5th floor we saw firemen everywhere. The 5th floor was a custodial area. It was dark and smoky. It reminded me of the original *Poseidon Adventure*, where the small group of survivors are trying to make their way to the hull of a ship that's been overturned. That's exactly what it was like. Broken pipes, hissing smoke. Water on the ground up to our ankles. The hallways were very narrow, lined with equipment lockers. It was so dark that we had to follow the lights affixed to the firemen's helmets or their flashlights for our next steps, or we would run into things. This was not the predictable terrain of the stairwells, with steps and stairwell platforms. Here John and I had to watch our every step to avoid sharp metal, wires, and exposed pipes. At each obstacle, we had to set the woman down, reposition ourselves, pick her up, and then carry her over debris. It was hard work, but what made it harder was the creeping suspicion that there was no discernible way out of the 5th floor.

The panic ratcheted up even higher. The yelling started again. "Why can't we get out!" people demanded. "C'mon, let's go! What's the problem? Tell us the problem!"

Some broke away from the firemen. I didn't think that that was a good idea. *Keep following the firemen.* We set out in another direction with one fireman and the small group of people still following him. We found a doorway off the custodial area where another fireman stood as if he was keeping watch. "Can we get out this way?" the fireman leading the way asked. The one in the doorway said, "No." John and I held the woman, and I watched these two firemen closely. "Why not?" said our fireman. The other fireman just shook his head and waved his hand as if to say, "Don't ask." There was no doubt in my mind now: Something had gone terribly wrong.

Looking back, I can only guess the fallout from the South Tower must have made it very dangerous to exit that doorway. Maybe there were bodies there. Who knows?

Now the little voice in my head was screaming: *We've got to get out of here NOW. We're stuck. I am definitely not in control of any of it anymore. We're not moving. We're on this dark floor. I have no idea where to turn for a way out. How the hell will the three of us get out of here?* I thought, if it came to it, I'd throw her over my shoulder and find some other way out of there.

We reversed course and followed the fireman back toward the very first exit we checked. People shouted their disapproval. "No, no—we already tried that way!" The fireman halted in his tracks. He turned and looked at all of us. We had arrived at that *Poseidon Adventure* moment where some people left the Reverend and some followed him. We followed. We chose well. We got to the doorway, and he said to us, "It's OK now. We can get out this way."

This stairwell was not like the one we had been using. The first thing we noticed was the almost-complete lack of other people. Earlier that could've been cause for alarm, but at this point, we saw it as a path with fewer obstacles. What made it different, but worse, was the lack of visibility, which made it almost impossible for us to keep a steady footing.

It was dark, smoky, and very slippery, with water everywhere. The only thing we could see and follow were the fluorescent glow strips on the stairs. That was enough. We flew down the last four flights of stairs to the lobby.

Through the Lobby, Out of the Building,
and Into the Ambulance

Like cave dwellers stepping cautiously into first light, we limped out from the dark stairwell and into the west side of the North Tower's lobby. We could see outside the building and out all the way to the West Side Highway. We made it. We were finally free from those damn stairs, from the confinement, from the lack of control. But our immediate sense of relief was quickly overcome by confusion resulting from a flood of new information as we surveyed the scene. To our right, toward the north end of the building, we saw devastation. It was a war zone. *What happened here? This is more than a transformer fire or a gas explosion.* Shattered glass littered the inside of the lobby and the outside of the building. Twisted metal poked out from all sides of the lobby walls, with chunks of broken cement and loose paper all over the ground. The bright sun now had a dusty film over it—like snow, but dirty, with a grayish white hue. People moved around aimlessly, bandaged and bloodied—seemingly looking for help, for a friend, for something they lost, for I don't know what.

Three of us held the woman—the fireman on the back, me on one side, and John on the other. For John and me, fatigue was no longer a factor. Whatever strain we felt gave way to the new world of sights and sounds we had now entered. In fact, after sixty-eight floors, we no longer thought of ourselves as two men carrying a woman in a wheelchair. The chair had become an unconscious extension of our own bodies—the three of us moving as one body. When we turned, she turned. If we bent low, she went low. When we froze—startled or shocked—she froze with us. The three of us—me, John, and the woman—had become incapable of moving anywhere except together.

We stood there gripping the chair, dazed, trying to make sense of what we were seeing. My eyes wandered to a fireman helping a woman walk through a window space in the lobby where there was no longer a window—totally surreal. Then I looked left and saw another fireman help a woman without shoes get over some debris and under the giant metal strip that once divided a massive pane of glass.

We were on our own. No one was telling us where to go. I'm sure we had that lost look on our faces. For a moment I was struck motionless. I stared out at the madness, semi-bewildered. One fireman approached us. It was as if he had read my thoughts. "Take her out past the corner over there. It's fully blown out," he barked. In the northwest corner of the lobby, even the metal strip was gone. The space was gutted. It looked as though the mammoth structures of glass and steel that girded the area had been completely and violently vacuumed out. My god. That morning—just about an hour and a half earlier—I'd clocked in for work in that exact same lobby.

The fireman, John, and I carried the woman through the broken window space and across to the West Side Highway area. Now where? The three of us scanned the area for any direction that looked more like safety than danger. The fireman helping us got a call on his radio. They wanted his location. "I'm helping a situation here," he told them. The situation was us.

Finally someone pointed us to an ambulance. We saw it facing south on the southbound side of the West Side Highway, right in front of the North Tower. We walked across the northbound side, across the divider, and presented the woman to the EMT guys at the ambulance. Amazingly, with all the destruction around us, the ambulance was empty.

They undid the Velcro straps, removed her from the evacuation wheelchair, and placed her in the back of the ambulance.

She started to cry. She hadn't cried at all the whole time we'd been together. In fact, throughout our entire journey, she'd shown little emotion at all. As soon as she was in the ambulance, she began to let it out. "Hey, what are you crying for?" I said to her. "Don't worry, everything is going to be fine." I thought maybe she was still worried about her motorized wheelchair. She motioned to me with her hands—tiny hands—to give her a hug. We embraced gently. I gave her my business card. "Listen," I said. "Don't worry. When I get back up there, I'll find your wheelchair." I backed out of the ambulance. The paramedic said, "Do you guys want to take the ride with us?" John and I looked at each other. We saw no need to do so. It seemed like the right decision for both of us.

About John

If I had to pick a partner to help me that day, there could have been no better person than John Cerqueira. He was a young kid who I knew had a good heart and good character and would do the right thing.

I hired John. I had interviewed him when he came up on spring break from North Carolina State. I didn't know that he was still in school when the interview was set up. He was a kid full of energy—very positive, with a confident outlook in life and the future. He was perfect sales material. At the time, we had just begun hiring kids straight out of college. "I like what I see," I'd told him. "You say all the right things. You look like you really want to do this. After you're done with graduation, come back up and interview with me again." He came back up at the end of May, and I hired him in June of 2001. Think about it. This kid from North Carolina had been working in the Towers for three months when all hell broke loose.

John's youth, energy, and good nature worked as the perfect complement to my instinct to navigate. While I was constantly looking for the next move and deciding which turn to take, John provided very positive vocal support to the woman—joking around, asking her what she needed. We were constantly trying to keep her level so she didn't fall. John would often shout to a third person helping us, "C'mon, we got to keep this level. She's falling!"

From the moment I met John in the stairwell to the moment we shut that ambulance door closed, he and I had been together, keeping an eye out for each other. We'd made sure to remain within reaching distance of each other, calling back if either of us lagged behind. When we got to the 68th floor, John followed me off the stairwell and into those offices. When I asked him to help me carry the woman in the wheelchair, I felt a little weird, like I was imposing. But John helped without hesitation. Now that we'd gotten her to relative safety and our hands were free, we stood in front of the ambulance and wondered, "Where do we go from here?"

Outside: Getting My Orientation

The ambulance pointed south. Watching the ambulance doors shut, we faced west with our backs to the devastation. At this point, I still had no idea about the enormity of the morning's events. I still didn't know exactly what had happened to my building, Tower 1. I thought a plane—a small plane—had hit us, or that there was some gas-related fire. As we got lower and lower down the stairs, I began to realize that something more dire had taken place. But what? I didn't know, nor had I considered that anything at all had happened to Tower 2.

Questions jumbled in my head. *Should I be finding my office-mates?* I stood there in the middle of the West Side Highway and turned around toward the Towers. I suddenly lapsed into a state of shock and disbelief. Dust and paper filled the air.

Shattered glass, mangled wires, and broken pieces of concrete and metal were everywhere. I stood still in front of the North Tower, my building. Just a few feet away from me, a giant piece of the building's façade had crashed into the ground. I stared up at Tower 1. It was still intact. I could see that the top of the building was on fire. It was a huge, raging fire. I checked myself. I wasn't completely shaken. I was just trying to take it all in. Even amid all this ruin, I didn't feel that my life was completely in danger. Hell, I was out of the building now and no longer carrying the woman in the wheelchair. I wasn't restricted at all. I was in control again. *I could run. No, I could walk out of this now.*

There weren't that many people outside. I shouted to someone walking by, "Where's this big piece from?" No response, only blank stares. They were walking around dazed. In retrospect, I bet most of them had seen the South Tower fall just minutes before. They didn't know I didn't know. Nobody directed us to get out of there because nobody knew what to do. Everyone was covered in a gray dust. And there were papers everywhere, so much paper.

All of this wreckage came from the implosion of Tower 2. But from where I was standing, I couldn't see Tower 2. Even if I could, I wouldn't have been able to comprehend that it was not there. There was so much to process, and none of it was making sense. If someone had sat me down and explained to me there was no more Tower 2, there's no way I could've been able to wrap my head around that fact. In my worldview, there was still a Tower 2, there were no terrorists, and no Osama bin Laden.

I tried to get my bearings. I looked for the Marriott Hotel, which was situated in between the two towers facing the West Side Highway. Some nights after work, we'd go to Tall Ships, the corner bar-restaurant in the hotel. The Marriott was there, all right. It looked as though the hand of a giant had smashed an equally giant arrow right through the middle of its roof. I had never seen anything like it.

Standing in front of the North Tower, I contemplated my next move. I started walking south because that's where it looked like there was more of the destruction. Maybe I could find out what really happened. After a few steps, a fireman in a white shirt stood in my way. He looked drawn. "Listen," he said, "if you go down that way, be prepared to see things you haven't seen before. Be prepared to see carnage."

"What? What are you talking about?"

He looked me in the face, and I saw all his sadness, resignation, seriousness, and resolve.

John, who had been standing next to me, immediately began walking in the opposite direction, walking north. His face had suddenly changed. He looked ill. "C'mon, Mike. I don't want to see dead people."

Dead people? Carnage? My brain couldn't accept it.

But what did I know? All my frames of reference were lost to me. It no longer sounded like New York City. I heard the fire burning and crackling on top of Tower 1 and a cacophony of screaming sirens, papers fluttering, voices here and there calling out to each other for help. All this set against an unusual silence much like the kind that takes over Manhattan on a snow-covered day when the city goes silent yet you can hear single noises.

Jolting me from my confusion, a fireman came running out of Tower 1, right in front of me, as if he'd just made it out in the nick of time. Another fireman rushed to help him with an urgency I hadn't seen in anyone in the few minutes I had been standing outside. They moved as if getting out now was a matter of life and death.

Then I heard sounds unlike the others. The strangeness of the sounds—sounds so foreign that I could not relate or associate them with anything my brain could define or visualize—distracted, but didn't frighten, me. In the context of everything else, the sounds were inherently suspicious. There was no familiar source like paper or sirens that I could match to them. They were loud, unpleasant thuds of singular things falling and hitting hard. I heard them one, two, sometimes three in a row. Then several seconds, maybe a minute, would pass; and I'd hear those sounds again. I wanted to know what they were, but I did not want to look. I knew these were not good things. *I just knew.*

Without a word, John peeled away from me again, walking farther north. Where was *he* going? The fireman's warning echoed in my head. *Do not go there unless you want to see things you've never seen before.* All of a sudden, this guy—a stranger—appeared in front of me.

I don't know who he was. I don't know why he was down there. He wasn't a fireman. He was a guy dressed in casual street clothes. Not too tall. Long brown hair, almost shoulder-length. Chiseled features. Sunken eyes. Around my age. He had a lightweight jacket on. "C'mon, Mike," he said to me. "I'll go with you down this way." He motioned south. And he called me by my name.

"What?" I said, feeling confused.

He said it again. "Really. C'mon, Mike. I'll go with you. Let's go down this way. C'mon, Mike." He said my name a few times. *Do I know this guy?* I looked at him—this stranger—and I thought for a second: *Should I go down that way—south? Maybe people need help. Or maybe I need to see what's really going on—see the things I "haven't seen before."*

I looked back over at John. I saw his chin go into his chest. He was sobbing. I looked at the guy, and I looked at John. I walked to John.

John said it again. "Mike, let's go. I don't want to see dead people." That's when it dawned on me. I looked up, and I saw them—people falling from Tower 1, my building, and hitting the lower roof of 6 World Trade Center. That's what those sounds were—the sounds I'd never heard before, and never want to hear again.

John had seen it and understood. So much had been falling from the sky I hadn't paid close attention to what the sounds were. They hadn't registered. Seeing John's reaction made it register. I saw then too clearly that it wasn't paper or debris. It was bodies. My brain and my emotions were completely overwhelmed. Unlike any other moment since this emergency began, there was no blocking this horrific reality out of my mind. This changed me.

Somewhere inside, I broke. I had no *reaction* for this. I looked at John with his head hanging. "Sure, let's go." I did not look back.

If I had gone south, I wouldn't be here today.

We walked north.

My head was spinning. *What the hell did I just see?* Things weren't making sense. That calm, disembodied voice was now an emergency signal. *I'm still here. I'm safe. I still don't know what went on here, but now I've got a burning question I need answered: What in God's name has happened here that people are falling from the sky?*

I couldn't process what I'd just seen. I couldn't accept it. I tried, but I couldn't. I lost focus. My ultra-sharp sense of *what's the next move* that was so acute inside the building had gone foggy. I was staggered, meandering.

We took a few steps north. My head was no longer on an alert swivel, but bowed. A cameraman must have seen me shaking my head in disbelief. He got close and said, "Tell me what you saw and heard." Incredibly, I related to him every material fact of my journey in a reasonably coherent manner: my name, my company, what floor I was on, what floor we found the woman in the wheelchair, that we put her in an ambulance.

People very well could've been watching this live at the time. It was probably around 10:25 a.m. or 10:26 a.m. The cameraman said thank you. John and I stepped clumsily over the rubble away from him. We didn't know it, but he kept filming us.

At one point during his questioning, I choked up. I couldn't stop thinking about those horrible images. I realized that yes, we're here, we're out of the building, but this is not a good situation. The entire day began to catch up to me. From the Network Plus office, to carrying the woman down, to the dark panic of the 5th floor, to the disorientation outside the building, the debris everywhere, the unthinkable things I witnessed—it was all coming together. I finally came to accept what I could not accept at any point before: *This is bad. Something awful and dangerous happened because people are dead, and I've seen people dying in front of me, and I don't know where anybody is. And whatever this awful danger is, it might still be happening.*

I could see the cameraman filming us from a distance. *Why is this guy filming us? What's the matter with him?* I shook my head and said the first wholly accurate thing I'd said all day: "It's chaos, man. This is chaos."

Without speaking, John and I took a few unsure steps north, away from the tower. Then I heard an explosion that made my whole body flinch. As if on reflex, I raised my hands to cover my ears and protect my head. I'll never forget actually feeling it coming up behind me on the back of my neck. It shook me out of my skin. It's almost as if someone had pushed me from the back. That's because the enormous explosion I heard was actually right behind me. I turned around, looked up, and saw the top of the North Tower erupting like a volcano. I thought it was going to come down right on top of me. One look was all I needed.

Real and abject fear took hold. *You fucked up! You waited around here too long. Now you're going to die.*

The basic instinct to move—the one I had inside the tower—screamed inside me. I instantly became reduced to nothing more than the sum of my instincts to survive. I took off running. Like a shot, I ran. You should know that I am fast. Very fast. I was all-area high school track in the 100 and 200 meters. A "fast white boy," they used to call me. This was the fastest I've ever run in my life. It was everyone for themselves. You knew you had to run to survive, and that was all you could do. John had been several yards ahead of me when the explosion hit. There were firemen around me. And the cameraman was well north of me.

I blew by John and the fireman. The cameraman stayed put, filming me running toward him. *What is he doing? He will die.* I kept running.

I felt a thunderous, rumbling force coming up from behind me, like a tidal wave of iron and wind. I couldn't see it, but I knew it was gaining fast. I knew it would hurt me if it caught me. And I knew I couldn't outrun it. Something would hit me or knock me into something else. Cover was my only way out. *Find cover!* This was surely a new kind of survival mode from the one I felt in the building. This was not simply next-move mode, but next move fueled by the certain knowledge that I was not invincible. I'd already seen death, and I could be killed.

There was no cover except for parked cars. I looked for one higher off the ground. I saw what looked like a welder's truck, and I made a beeline for it. I cut right in front of someone to get to it. I don't know who it was. I didn't know where John was. All I knew was this stuff, this tornado of debris and crap, was literally at my heels. I felt it. I had no choices left. I threw my torso under the truck with my feet hanging out curbside.

As I lay under the truck, a wave of dust and debris washed over me, consuming every free space of air. I braced myself for impact, for pain, for whatever would happen to me. The debris blew over me, pounding and nicking against the metal truck. People were screaming. Someone landed on top of me, on my backside and legs. Were they alive? I called out, but there was no answer. And then everything went black—completely black. I couldn't breathe. I was gasping from running, so I needed air. I took a breath. It was like sucking ash from a fireplace. It choked me. It was like being underwater. I took tiny breaths, but that was no use either. All the air was gone. A minute ago it was a beautiful, clear day; and now I could not see my hand in front of my face. I couldn't see any detail of anything. Just blackness.

This is the time I'd rather forget. This was my bottom. My mind jumped from one dark corner to another. *I'm in one piece, but I can't breathe and I can't see. No one knows where I am. None of my family. Not Joy. I can't be here. How will they look for me? How would they find me?* I wasn't accepting my own death yet. But brief and terrifying thoughts flashed in my head about things that could happen that I had no control over. My means of survival were cut off. Just like at the stairwell, I was stuck. I was at a total loss. I couldn't run. Even if I could run, where to? It was pitch black! Mentally I tiptoed along the fine line of refusing to give in and fearing that something could hit me that I didn't see coming. I hated the idea that nobody knew where I was and no one I knew was around. It was an empty feeling. *Is this how it ends? Alone?* I started blaming myself. I was too nonchalant when I got out of the building. I should've said, "We got her in the ambulance, now let's get the hell out of here." *What was I thinking? If I had just gotten out of there then, I'd be farther away. I'd be out of this danger.*

I searched for my old voice again. *Try to stay calm. Get back in survival mode. Get rational.* I still couldn't breathe. *What can you do? OK, I'm in a fire, with smoke. You're not supposed to breathe it in. Stay low. Stay calm. Wait to breathe again.* I called out for John with a short breath. "John!" I thought maybe it was him who landed on me. I wanted to know if he, whoever he was, was OK.

He didn't answer. I said it again. "Hey, Johnny?" No answer. "Hey, Johnny?" Still no answer. I was thinking maybe he was dead or unconscious. Then I heard a strong, steady voice. "Just stay down," the voice said. "It'll pass. Just stay down." The voice was right. The blackness started to dissipate. It went from black to dark gray, but I still didn't move from under that truck. I tried to stay calm and hold my breath for as long as I could.

Then I heard someone call out, "Mike . . . Ben! Hey, Mike?" It was John, coughing uncontrollably. He got up way too soon. But he was behind a van where people were pulling at him and grabbing him, saying, "Help me, I'm dying." He had to get away from there.

The person that landed on me turned out to be a fireman. He was aiming for the same spot under the truck, but I got there first. But he got his head down under the truck, lying on top of me. He was the one to tell me it would pass. He got up, tapped my back, and said, "Attaboy, you'll be OK. *We're* OK."

I was under that truck for only a few minutes, but it felt like a lot longer. Still on all fours, I put my hand up to signal John. I couldn't speak because I had all this crap in my throat. John was wearing something over his face. I didn't want to touch my face because I thought it might make things worse.

A rescue worker seemed to be coming toward me. He had a helmet on and an oxygen tank on his back. I was down on my hands and knees, coughing this stuff out of my lungs. I looked up wide-eyed at the rescue worker. Somebody pointed to me and yelled, "This guy needs oxygen!"

The rescue worker looked at me, but there was nothing behind his eyes. The poor guy was walking around in shock. He didn't give me any oxygen. He didn't give anyone any oxygen. He walked toward me with a vacant expression. I looked at him, and I didn't really care about the oxygen. I understood. God knows what he went through.

I stood up. John was OK. I was OK. We started to walk away.

When you watch the video of me trying to outrun the imploding North Tower, you can clearly see from a wider perspective the tremendous force of dust and rubble that knocked people down. You'll see people literally flying, blown in the air across the street. Seeing that, I realize how close I was. Anything could have happened. I could've been mortally wounded in any number of ways. I could've gotten knocked forward and slammed my head into a fire hydrant or a car or whatever, and I'd be dead. I could have gotten pinned down under that truck, knocked unconscious and suffocated in the blackness. I could have simply tripped while running and never even made it to shelter of any kind. Who knows? I think of the people during the tsunami in Asia who were able to somehow survive the initial catastrophic tidal wave and were strong enough to handle the floodwaters but were killed by a snakebite. On 9/11 it didn't matter that I was fast or strong or alert. I was lucky. That's all it was.

Walking Uptown

We looked for water. The Red Cross had set up an emergency outpost truck in the middle of the West Side Highway, less than one hundred yards north of where I dove for cover. They stopped us, sat us down, and gave us some water. Many people stopped there. We couldn't sit still. As we walked away, heading north, a woman who identified herself as a *New York Times* reporter started interviewing us. We must've looked like good subjects because the entire exteriors of our bodies—our clothes, hands, hair, and face were covered with ash and dust. A Hasidic man approached us, looking annoyed. He saw the way we looked and that nobody was helping us, yet this woman was pushing for an interview. He interrupted the interview. "Come over here," he said to me. He pulled me aside. He grabbed a bottle of water, washed out my eyes, and cleaned my face. I don't know who this man was, but if I saw him today, I'd give him a big, big hug. What a moment of perspective. He saw me. He saw that I obviously just came out of the mess. I've got crap all over my face. The man thinks, *Why doesn't someone help him clean up because as you can see, he can't do it for himself?* So he took the time to wash my face. It was a pure, kind, humane act—seeking nothing but the act itself. *Kindness.* In fact, it was the first time anyone had extended physical aid to me since I first felt the explosion on the 81st floor. And for the first time since the beginning of it all, I dropped my need for control and allowed someone else to offer me direction and aid.

The reporter continued with her interview. I got annoyed too, a little, but she was the first one to tell us anything.

The reporter asked, "Do you know what's going on?" We said no.

I didn't know either of the Towers had imploded. Even when I was running for my life and then dove under the truck, my mind was only thinking, *Survive, get out of this.* Now I learned that both towers were gone.

I thought back to just moments earlier when I had gotten out of the building. I didn't really see the South Tower, did I?

I thought at the time that it was simply hard to see well with all the dust and debris and the smoke. Maybe it was just where I was standing at the time, I thought, so I wasn't able to see the South Tower. I certainly wasn't associating the façade debris I saw with a completely imploded South Tower. And nobody down near where we were—so close to the site—was talking about the South Tower imploding.

The reporter continued her explanation. There were "acts of terrorism." She said she thought there was one or two more hijacked planes still up in the air, unaccounted for.

This altered my entire perspective. *This was an attack on our country, and we're still not safe because there are two more planes up there?*

My mind was racing. *I've got to find people. I have to talk to my family. I have to talk to Joy. I've got to make sure everybody is OK.* I still couldn't entirely grasp what kinds of planes did this or what had really happened.

We needed to find phones. We left the reporter and continued walking along the West Side Highway to a sanitation building, four blocks from the site. People were constantly stopping and staring at us. We were a mess. We were covered in soot and partially wet, thanks to the kind man who washed our faces. We looked like we'd literally been through hell, if hell was covered in gray ash. The sanitation workers said we could use their bathrooms. What we really wanted was their office phones because our cell phones weren't working. That was fine with them. John and I sat at desks on different sides of their office and dialed.

I called my parents. I couldn't get through. John got through to his parents, and I heard him sob, getting bits and pieces of information to them.

On the third try, I got through. My brother, Angelo, picked up.

"Michael?" I heard a tinge of desperation and relief in his voice.

"Anj, it's me."

"Michael, are you OK?"

I could hear him, but he couldn't hear me too well.

"Michael," he spoke slowly and deliberately. "ARE YOU OK?"

"I'M FINE."

I faintly heard a cheer in the background. Then it hit me. I was overcome with emotion. I did everything I could to hold back from pouring my emotions out all over the sanitation office floor. If I kept the conversation going, I would lose it.

"Anj, I'm fine. I'll call you right back."

The last time my family heard from me was when I called my dad from the 55th floor at approximately 9:15 a.m. I told him then I'd call when I got out. In the meantime, they saw both towers go down. They couldn't get in touch because cell phones didn't have signals. My tower, the North Tower, went down at 10:28 a.m., and I did not call them until about forty minutes later. God knows what they went through. Forty minutes became an eternity.

But what's forty minutes? So many people did not know the fate of their loved ones for hours, days. And today, for many— far too many—there's still no word, no finality, just speculation, absence, and utter loss.

It was around 11:15 a.m. when I hung up with my brother.

I called Joy next; I got through. "Hey sweets" was all we got out before the phone went dead. But she got it. She knew I was OK. And I knew that the most important people in my life knew I was OK.

No sooner had we walked out the door of the sanitation building than we saw a mob of people running toward us up the West Side Highway. Emergency vehicles, fire trucks, a police car zoomed north, racing past us. The chaos was back. Like a conditioned reflex, we started running. That was hard for John because he had injured his ankle earlier. *This is crazy! When is it going to stop?* Exasperated, I yelled to whoever was listening: "What the hell's going on?" Someone shouted back that a gas leak was going to explode any minute. John said, "Mike, I can't run anymore."

"Enough!" I said. We got off the West Side Highway and started weaving our way in, toward the city's interior. At Gansevoort Street in the Meatpacking District, we saw people huddled outside a storefront window watching TV like people did when Neal Armstrong landed on the moon. We stopped to watch some of it. I couldn't believe my eyes. What I saw was a huge airliner flying into the World Trade Center.

It had to be a movie clip. I still wasn't completely buying everything I was hearing: terrorist attacks, the Pentagon, planes still out there.

Cell phone service came back. Joy and I traded phone calls as I slowly progressed north. I didn't want to talk on the phone for long because there was too much going on. I had to keep moving. I told her I would find her later uptown. She had gone from Atlantic Records to her friend Robert Finkman's place on the Upper East Side at 81st and 2nd avenues.

Then Boozer called. He said to come to his office, his exterminating business on 30th and Broadway. That was my next stop.

John and I continued up to 14th Street, moving east between 9th and 8th avenues, where we came upon an old but regal brown brick church, the Roman Catholic Church of St. Bernard. "Do you want to go in, Mike?" John said. I nodded in assent. John and I walked up the steps slowly. There were some people sitting on them. They were praying for their friends. Like so many others we'd passed on our walk so far, they could tell by looking at us where we'd been. "You were there," someone in a red T-shirt said. We told them we were in Tower 1.

"We're worried about our buddies. We are trying to figure out if they are OK.'"

"Where were they?" I asked

"They were in the North Tower too."

"What company did they work for?"

"Cantor Fitzgerald."

"What floor is that?"

They said 100th or 101st.

I searched for something to say, but I found nothing. I remembered the flames above my head on my 81st-floor corner office. And I certainly remembered seeing the top of the North Tower exploding. I looked at the group and didn't say a word. The one in the red T-shirt looked me in the eyes. He knew. I didn't know for sure what had happened to their friends, but I knew it couldn't be good. What words could I say? I walked into the church.

The church was almost empty, and very quiet. A woman sat alone in the front pew to the left. We walked straight up the center aisle. There was an altar front and center and a cross to the right. John knelt down in front of the cross and was praying intensely. I went into a pew to my right. I was exhausted. I got down on my knees and said, "God, I don't know what I did to be in your good graces, but thank you." John came beside me, and we knelt there together in silence for a while.

I was raised Catholic, an altar boy for seven years, and received all the sacraments during that time. I went to church almost every Sunday in those days. As an adult, I practiced my faith infrequently. But I made myself a promise I would go every Sunday from that time on.

We left the church and headed to Boozer's office. Along the way we passed various restaurants with outdoor seating, where, to my astonishment, people were sipping cocktails and snacking on hors d'oeuvres and, well, just eating lunch. *What the hell?* They were chatting and pulling at the waiter as if it was just another sunny September Tuesday in Manhattan. I think about that image today, and I still can't believe it.

Boozer

Boozer is Brian Wenrich. He owns Quinn Exterminating on 30th and Broadway, located on the "penthouse" floor of an old eight-story building. His father was a high school football coach at Our Lady of the Valley in Orange, New Jersey. As a boy, Brian was a stocky kid with big calves. He hung around his dad's football practices, anxious to participate with the older boys. The high school players nicknamed him after Emerson Boozer, a straight-ahead fullback for the New York Jets in the 1970s. As Boozer got older, the nickname became more apt, owing to his jovial consumption of alcoholic libations. I met Boozer in a softball league when I was twenty-six. I'm surprised we hadn't met earlier. We are the same age, born twelve days apart. We grew up in neighboring towns, me in Montclair and he in Essex Fells. He went to public school, and I went to a Catholic school, and our paths didn't cross. But we hit if off as soon as we met. Kindred spirits, we were. We bonded as single guys enjoying their run-and-gun years. We went to concerts, ball games, and bars. We became like brothers. For the two years I had been working in New York, I met him for lunch once or twice a week a block from his office at O'Reilly's, a great old New York City drinking establishment. I also made Quinn Exterminating a customer, which was not only good business but also a convenient excuse to visit with him during the workweek.

Boozer would give you the shirt off his back. And on this day, that's literally what I needed.

When John and I walked into Boozer's building, the security guys gave us the *What the hell you must've been through* look everybody everywhere gave us. They stared at us like we were ghosts. We entered Quinn Exterminating, and Boozer's assistant gave us the same look.

The door to Boozer's office was open. I edged a few feet away from the door and watched him without saying a word. He stood there, focused intently on a little TV set, propped up on an office chair, that showed the catastrophe—the planes hitting, the Towers imploding—over and over again. Sensing eyes on him, he wheeled around and gave me a big bear hug.

"Boozer, I'm a mess."

"Man, I don't care. You're fucking *alive*."

The little TV set drew me in. I watched a clip of the second plane crashing into Tower 2. It was the first time that day I really saw what happened. I know people had told me about the terrorists and the planes, but it was all still inexplicable to me. "Boozer, what's going on?"

Boozer explained to me all that he knew. It was a lot to take in.

As Boozer told me the tale of two planes and how the Towers were no more, my cell phone regained service. From then on it would ring nonstop. Things got hectic. I was working two phones at once. I took calls on the cell phone with one hand and made calls on Boozer's office phone with the other.

I got through to my CEO around 1:00 p.m. The Network Plus home office was making a head count. No one had spoken to me yet. I told him John Cerqueira was with me. John looked up quizzically. Then Tom Sullivan called. Sully is a college buddy who lives out in Colorado. He was very upset, crying. He said he saw me on TV. He saw me running up the West Side Highway live on the news, and then everything turned to black on the screen. He thought I didn't make it. He had been trying to reach me for the past hour and a half. "I thought you were gone," he said.

I talked to Joy again. I called my parents' house again. Apparently, a lot of people were calling my parents' house.

"We got to get you out of those clothes," Boozer said.

Boozer gave me and John exterminator outfits—gray pants, a gray shirt with the Quinn Exterminating logo, and some sneakers. I peeled off everything: shirt, tie, T-shirt, pants. I threw all of it in the trash. I learned later that Boozer took it out of the trash and put it in a plastic bag for me. He gave it to me a couple weeks later. I did not open that bag until I began to write this book. That gray ashlike dust, and that smell—that acrid burning scent that I'd never smelled before and never smelled since—are still on those clothes. I still don't know quite what to do with them.

I felt better sitting in Boozer's office in clean clothes. I had also been brought up to speed. I understood what had happened at the World Trade Center. I knew about the Pentagon. I knew there was still one plane unaccounted for. That's the story we were following. The phone continued to ring.

Joy was waiting for me uptown. I was at 30th and Broadway. She was at 82th and 2nd. But I knew she was OK, and she knew I was OK. The overwhelming sense of urgency that dominated the last three hours—the longest three hours of my life—had left me. As long as I knew everybody was OK, I relaxed, mentally. Or maybe that was the feeling I wanted to have, so I gave it to myself, just temporarily. How long could I stay in emergency mode?

"Let's get you something to eat and drink," Boozer recommended. So John, Boozer, and I walked over to O'Reilly's. Normally, we sat at the bar to eat, but the bar was packed. The

whole place was packed. Boozer found us some space in the
back, in the dining area where patrons enjoy the frill of white
tablecloths. This was the first time I'd sat anywhere but at the
bar at O'Reilly's. Boozer ordered us beers and a ton of food. I
didn't realize it, but I was starving. I was insatiable. I had beers
in each hand. I was so keyed up, so intense and full of energy
that I could've consumed anything and I wouldn't have felt it
at all. I was full of adrenaline, antsy, unable to sit still. I guzzled
beer, not to escape or get drunk, but to simply feel the liquid. I
devoured one cheeseburger and then another. Boozer continued
to fetch food for us from the front bar.

I was inhaling a fistful of fries when Boozer called to me to
come to the front. And there I was, on TV. I watched the clip
of me running for my life up the West Side Highway. *It's about
2:30 p.m. Four hours earlier, this was all actually happening. Now
I'm watching it on TV!* This was hard to process. "That's me,"
I said sotto voce with some disbelief. It was surreal, and it was
frightening all over again.

That was it. Like a lightning bolt, sanity hit me. *I've gotta get
the hell out of here and go see Joy.*

I thanked Boozer for his incredible friendship and generosity.
What better wise man could this wanderer have chosen?

John and I started back out on foot and soon after caught a bus
heading uptown on 5th Avenue. The driver was not accepting
fares. He took us as far as the corner of Central Park South, right
in front of the Plaza Hotel on 59th Street. I remember thinking
about the bizarre opulence of this New York City landmark
juxtaposed against the cataclysmic wreckage I'd been inside not
long ago.

There were twenty-nine more blocks and several avenues to go
to get to Joy on 88th and 2nd. With John and me back on foot, I
got another call from corporate saying that a reporter from *USA*

Today wanted to interview me. "Yeah, fine, whatever," I said. My mind was in a million places. I couldn't think straight. "Is it all right if we give out your cell phone number?" they asked. I was apprehensive but had no time to evaluate this. "Yeah, sure. Look, I gotta go."

Two blocks later, at around 4:30 p.m., my cell phone rang. It was the guy from *USA Today*. He said, "I heard what you did . . ." Blah, blah, blah. "Is it all right if we talk now?"

I don't care. Fine. OK. The reporter was very nice. He patiently asked questions. He listened. He seemed to really get it. According to my cell phone records, it was a forty-five-minute interview. I passed the phone to John, and they talked for a while too.

He asked me some personal questions about my religion. I told him I was an altar boy for seven years. He asked about my physical ability, wanting to know how I could carry the woman down sixty-eight flights. I told him I played college football and rugby. He was pretty thorough.

The next day, Tuesday, September 12, the interview ran prominently in the front page of the Money section in *USA Today*. I can only guess he found out about us from the video clip that ran that day. The article didn't mention whether the woman we carried out was alive. He didn't know, and neither did we.

Billy

As soon as the interview ended, the phone rang again. It was another college pal from Brown, Billy Hayes. "Harry, what do you need? Where are you?" Billy lived on the Upper West Side.

"Billy, I need a shirt, a jacket, and a hat."

"I don't care where you are, Harry. Whatever you need, I'm bringing it to you."

I gave him my location and told him my final destination: Joy at 88th and 2nd.

"You keep going where you're going," Billy said. "I'll catch up with you."

At 72nd Street, John and I cut over from 5th Avenue to 2nd Avenue. The phone never stopped ringing. It felt like all I was doing was walking and talking.

We hit 88th and 2nd. I turned the corner to go to Robert's building, and I ran smack into Billy. He was there with a hat, a jacket, and a shirt.

"You OK?"

"Yeah, I'm OK."

"C'mon, come with me to this bar over here," he said, pointing to Cronies on 2nd Avenue.

"I'm on my way to see Joy. She's waiting for me, Billy."

"Here, take this stuff. We'll wait right here for you."

As I walked away from Billy, things went a little numb. I didn't feel fatigued or pumped with adrenaline. Now I was just moving. It didn't matter what direction. I'd see Joy in a minute—in thirty seconds. *My fiancée. My Joy. I will touch her hand and connect back to myself, back to something else, back to clarity and decisiveness and sanity and equilibrium. I'm moving, and I will not stop moving until I see Joy.*

We entered the building lobby. Joy came bouncing down the steps. She couldn't wait to see me. I wanted to embrace her. But I didn't. Or I couldn't. She wanted to give me a big hug, but I pulled back. To this day, I don't know what came over me. I was aloof, almost formal. "How are you doing?" I asked her. I made stiff introductions. "This is John. This is Joy."

Joy says she looked in my eyes, and there was nobody there. I was gone.

This was supposed to be like a scene out of the movies, where the music swells and the man and the woman have that big emotional reunion after being apart for the entire heart-stopping ordeal. I don't know if I wanted it to be that way. Maybe I didn't want to feel some things. I didn't want to accept the madness I'd witnessed, the severity of where I'd been. I didn't want to feel the reality. It was too much to relive right away, too much to reflect on. I didn't want to accept that I was that close to death and almost didn't make it. Showing great emotion would be to acknowledge that great emotion was warranted, which meant accepting the thing that caused it—the hell I had been through. It meant I had to accept the terrible feeling I had while trapped under that truck, in the blackness, suffocating and thinking I might not see Joy ever again. Hours had passed since I was under that truck. I had had time to put it out of my head. I couldn't reverse the slight peace of mind I had found. I couldn't relive this thing emotionally with her right then and there. I wanted normalcy. I wanted distance from it—distance from my true feelings about what I experienced. I didn't want to be overwhelmed anymore. I didn't want another moment today where I would be relinquishing control. By fending off my own emotions, I disabled myself from feeling and showing emotion to Joy, the person with whom I truly wanted to share my deepest feelings. At that moment, I began to build walls. It was a building project that would continue for years.

We went upstairs. Robert had prepared lovely crudités—delicate finger foods—and champagne. He lived in a studio apartment. He never kept much in his apartment anyway. He likely put together whatever he had in the fridge.

Of the innumerable surreal moments of the day, this one topped them all. I took a napkin and began to eat. I felt myself swirling in a daze. I could barely follow the conversation in the room. John was doing a lot of talking. I collected myself for a minute and noticed I was drinking a glass of champagne. My god, what the hell was happening?

I took a shower. John took a shower.

I put on a pair of Robert's pants; the shirt, jacket, and hat Billy brought me; and a pair of Boozer's sneakers. "Let's go out," I awkwardly suggested. I badly wanted out, mostly out of my own skin.

We met up with Billy Hayes and his friends at Cronies, a loud sports bar with a large, open front window area and what seemed like a TV for every patron. There stood Billy, at the corner of the long bar that stretched almost to the entrance, looking at me the same way he had the last twenty years, with a wise-ass grin that made me feel like I'd known him all my life. I had for most of it anyway. It seemed as though fate conspired to always keep us together.

Billy and I were freshman roommates at Brown, but we'd actually met a year earlier at a coin toss on the 50-yard line of a high school football game. I was a captain for Immaculate Conception High School, and he was a captain for Chatham Borough. It was a tough, close game. My team won.

We both got accepted to Brown. Schools often try to match up jock roommates. I got a note over the summer that my roommate was another football player, but at the last minute, he switched to another school. So they placed me with someone on the waiting list. He and I were complete opposites. Let's just say he was a bit more interested in his studies than I was. Billy lived in a better dorm on the other side of campus. His assigned roommate got killed in a boating accident off Long Island over the summer before school started, so Billy lived by himself. Days into the fall semester, my roommate got in a car accident. The poor guy took it as an opportunity to move out of our room to a dorm closer to his classes. In the locker room during the first week of freshman football, Billy approached me and said, "Aren't you Mike Benfante who I played against in high school?"

"You mean who you *lost* against in high school?"

Before either of us got stuck with new roommates, Billy moved in with me. We played football and rugby together and became best buddies. Billy was always a funny guy. He had a good heart and always knew how to have a good time. Our parents kidded each other. Mine hoped Billy would rub off on me. His hoped I would rub off on him. We did rub off on each other, much like two experienced bank robbers sharing the same cell. But we had fun. I learned to count on Billy for whatever I needed, whenever I needed it—no matter what the circumstances for either of us. 9/11 was no different. Who else would I run into that night but Billy?

The bar offered little relief. TVs in all four corners replayed the horror of the day over and over again. I watched every bit of it. And I drank and drank and drank—not for pleasure or for thirst, but because it was there. I consumed whatever was in my path. I was so charged up, and I couldn't come down. I was surrounded by people who cared about me—people I knew— yet I felt like an alien, isolated. I felt on edge. Before I knew it, the clock said 2:00 a.m.

Robert had already gone back to his apartment. John rose to leave. He said he could stay with a friend. I told him he could stay with us but that it was a small apartment. (Robert actually gave Joy and me his bed, and he slept on the couch.) We looked at each other like one-hundred-year-old friends. We hadn't been separated since we met on the stairwell early that morning. What was there to say? We were beyond words, beyond emotion, and beyond our own comprehension of what we'd been through together. "I'll call you tomorrow, first thing," I said. "I know you will, Mike," he said. And he left. We all left soon after.

On the walk back to Robert's, I started feeling woozy. Not drunk, but spent. I sat down on the building's stoop. I didn't want to move. Joy urged me to come upstairs. I finally obliged. I lay down and mumbled, "Hey Robert, if you have a bucket, put it by the bed." My head rested against the pillow, and I looked at Joy, her gorgeous brown eyes looking down at me. The next thing I knew, it was 5:00 a.m. I snapped up, totally awake. I never wake up like that, not that early.

I felt completely awake, clear, and conscious. Joy lay sleeping beside me. The forces of memory and disbelief mixed uneasily in my head, formulating a sad, simple question: Could this all have been real? I was also feeling upset, as if suddenly awakened from a nightmare. Finally, one thought so strong and definite blared at the front of my skull: *I gotta get out of here. Now.*

PART III

NOW WHAT?

WEDNESDAY, SEPTEMBER 12, 2001

I tapped Joy, quietly. "C'mon, let's go get coffee."

Robert was still sleeping. We left the apartment and walked east toward 1st Avenue. I'd never been in New York when it was so quiet. No cars, no horns, no buses, no planes. Nothing. It was like the Twilight Zone. All you heard was the occasional hum of the fighter jets flying above, patrolling the city.

It was early. A morning haze dulled the sun. We grabbed some bagels and coffee and walked all the way to the East River promenade, where we ate our breakfast and talked. I tried to express my feelings. I told her how happy I was that we were together and safe. I tried to explain that I was still feeling a bit over-whelmed by all that had happened. She said she understood and was very sympathetic. Then, quite suddenly, I was overcome by the urge to see my family. I wanted to leave the city as quickly as possible and go to them in New Jersey.

We returned to Robert's, gathered our things, thanked him, and left. It was 6:30 a.m. We heard that nothing was running—no trains, no buses. But the desire to see my family became all-consuming. Nothing was going to keep me from finding a way.

I flagged down a cab on 3rd Avenue. The cabbie rolled down his window to talk. I said to him in all earnestness, "This is very important. I need your help. Can you drive me to New Jersey?" He started screaming at me in broken English, "Do you know what's going on? Do you have any idea what happened yesterday? The tunnels and bridges are closed. What's the matter with you? I can't go to *New Jersey!*"

Joy and I laughed. So much for a Kumbayah moment. Did I know what happened? he asked. *Yes, my friend. I know what happened.*

We learned the PATH was running out of 33rd Street, so we made our way down there.

Nobody talked on the PATH that morning. Everyone had this far-off look in their eyes. It felt like we were all saying the same thing: "Did yesterday really happen?"

We got out of the PATH in Jersey City and walked directly to my car. It was parked outside of my apartment, but I wasn't going in. I walked right by it.

Joy went to her place to gather some things. Then we hopped in the car and drove to Verona. I pulled up at my parents' house around 8:00 a.m.

Wednesday in Verona

At my family's house, my parents occupied the lower half, and my sister's family lived on the top floor. I entered downstairs and caught my dad walking through the folding doors that led to the living room. Our eyes met. And he just shook his head. He was worn out, emotionally spent from the previous day's hell. He wrapped his arms around me, and we gave each other a big bear hug. With tears welling up, he held me by my shoulders. "You don't know how great it is to see you," he said. We cried some. We didn't speak much. He just shook his head a lot. And we stood there, together.

I can only imagine what he went through after speaking to me while I was on the 55th floor and then watching the Towers go down and having to sit back and wait and watch and not know and not be able to do a thing about it. My father was shaken up.

In some ways, I went through less than my family did. I knew they were safe. I knew about my own safety. But when I woke up that morning, the urge to see my family was overwhelming and immediate. By Wednesday morning, it had begun to sink in how close I came to never seeing them again. Also, I thought about what they were going through *because of me.* I felt responsible, like I put them through it. It hurt me to imagine their pain. It still hurts me to think about that.

Television news was on round the clock in my parents' living room, just like it was in every other house in America. As the day progressed, I slowly pieced together a more comprehensive picture of what happened the day before—the enormity of it, the loss of lives, the firemen, two planes, the Pentagon, the plane going down in Pennsylvania. My feeling responsible gradually gave way to feeling grateful. This was a historic event. While it was happening, I wasn't thinking, *This is one of the most devastating events in American history,* but it's now considered the worst-ever attack on American soil. It's compared to Pearl Harbor because it was a surprise attack, because of the number of lives lost and the frantic hurry to save people. But I saw no historical, political, or monumental significance. As I sat there and watched news commentators and politicians place the event in context—the *whys* and *hows* of it—all I could think was, *This was a terrible thing, and I happened to be in the middle of it.* That's it. There have been other disasters like this—both natural and man-made—in which people found themselves as involuntary participants. That's just the way it is. I just happened to be one of those people for this disaster. I also happened to be one of those people to get out safely. I'm still amazed at how lucky I was.

My father and I sat on the couch for a little while. I questioned him about what he knew. We watched the endless loop of destruction footage. He stood up in front of the TV and said, "There it is. You want to see it? There it is." Oh, how it must have made him go mad watching it over and over and over again. And they just kept showing it. He didn't want to see that image anymore. But you couldn't turn on the damn TV without seeing it.

When he watched those images on TV, he watched it from the perspective of a father who saw both towers collapse and knew his son was in there somewhere. He listened to the reports of how many lives were lost, how many firemen died, endless stories of individual loss and grief. Once I gave him a hug, I began to feel better, but I wanted to make sure he was OK, and that he could move on. 9/11 was a traumatic experience for him.

I went upstairs to see my oldest sister, Susan. I don't know if she fully grasped the situation, but it didn't matter. I hugged her, and I was so purely happy to see her face.

My mother was at Verona High School, where she worked managing the cafeteria. I drove up to the high school with Joy. Mom was right there as soon as I walked through the back doors of the school. She tried to be strong, but she cried as soon as she saw me. We gave each other a long hug, and then we walked around a little bit. She proudly introduced me to some co-workers. I stayed only a short time and then drove back with Joy to my family's house.

I saw my sister Maria later in the day. She had been at work and was emotionally exhausted. No melodrama. This was too heavy for that. You just had to be in their shoes. It's still hard for me to tell exactly what my family went through, but they went through more than anyone should.

As much as they might've wanted to know about me, what was important to me was to know about *them*. I wanted to know what everyone else was doing when it happened. "What were you doing when you heard? How did you react?" Mostly, it deflected their attention away from asking me questions. I didn't want to explain it all then.

My parents didn't probe me about that day, and I didn't want to tell them too much. My parents were world-class worriers, and they didn't need to know how close I came to such horror and death. I didn't want them to have to think about what I had gone through. Just being together was all any of us wanted or needed to know.

Angelo's House

That afternoon, I took a ride over to my brother's house. Angelo lived a half mile from my parents. He was in Upstate New York on business and wasn't due back for a couple more days. I saw his wife, Lisa; my three-year-old niece, Amanda; and my godson, Angelo Jr., who was just four months old. Lisa gave me a big hug and cried. Little Amanda was glued to the TV. She couldn't understand why we were acting so funny. She's thirteen years old now and still has never asked me about 9/11. None of my nieces or nephews do. I sat down on the couch in my brother's living room. Lisa handed me my godson. And then from nowhere, a calm washed over me. This child in my arms made me feel sane for the first time since it all happened. I sat still with him. I just sat. Joy says that was the only time the look in my eyes changed from distance and blankness to the look in the eyes of the person she knew when she first met me.

I felt love. I felt comfort. I felt peace. This was what life was supposed to be about. I don't know how long I held Angelo Jr., but it was for a while. And for that brief while, the madness stopped.

Lisa took little Angelo away to feed him. I sat with Amanda in front of the TV. The news was on. I became gripped by a report about the firemen. They said something about three hundred missing, or dead. And I lost it. I cried openly for the first time. I didn't want my niece to see me, so I got up from the couch and walked out to the back deck. I put my head in my hands. Joy tried to comfort me, but I was inconsolable. I just sobbed and sobbed.

The firemen they were talking about—I saw them. I remember their faces. These men were going up the stairs as I was going down. To remember those men, their faces, and know they didn't make it out filled me with a sadness I had never felt before. Tremendous anger would come later. But at that point, there was heavy, overwhelming sadness.

I felt for their families. Here I was, able to be with my family—my parents, my sisters, my niece, and my infant nephew—and there were so many people who were not having this same experience of reunion. Their houses and hearts were not full of joy and relief and people hugging, but were instead filled with sadness and longing and loss. In the days to follow, I couldn't get around that sadness. I couldn't stop thinking about the people who didn't make it out and what their families were going through. It makes me angry today to think of what these families *still* go through.

How do you not feel guilt? I was inside Tower 1 for ninety-six minutes after the plane hit. And I made it out—walked out—while rescue workers were still going *in*. Firemen charged *in*, knowing two planes had hit and/or knowing the other tower had already fallen. *They went in knowing this.* They went in to save other people. They didn't make it out, and I did. How can you not feel guilt? These are the same firemen that moved aside so I could carry a woman in a wheelchair around stairwell corners and out to safety. How can you not feel guilt? I get to spend time with my family, then and now, and they do not.

Today, I meet people at events having to do with 9/11, and it's difficult. Months after 9/11, I attended a dinner honoring me for what I did that day, and I met a father whose son did not make it out. He sought me out and embraced me. He told me about his son. And all I could feel was guilt. I feel connected to these people, but it's a different kind of connection. All the families that lost someone share a connection with each other that's completely different from the one they share with me. When I meet them and I tell them I was there on the 81st floor and I made it out—never mind anything else I did—they must be thinking, in the most natural, non-envious way, Why you and not my son, my daughter, my husband? When I see them, I tread very lightly because you just don't know what they're going through.

* * *

I thanked Lisa, left Angelo's house, and went back to my parents' in time to meet my mother, who was returning home from work. And then the calls started again.

NPR called. They wanted to do a phone interview. I didn't know it was live. I spewed out my story. NPR got me while I was still raw—still in shock—and intensely describing every detail of my experience. Many people heard that interview. I have a cousin in North Carolina who called and said he heard it. Friends from all over the country heard it. They were amazed at what I went through. As soon as I hung up, I got a call from CBC in Canada. Another phone interview. My cell phone was unlisted, but because my father and I share the same name, they were finding me through my parents. Friends and family were calling. I was on the phone a lot.

I was surprised by all the media attention. I didn't think it was a big story, just one of many. Everybody who was there had an amazing story to tell.

I ate dinner at my parents' house; then Joy and I spent the night at Angelo's. I had no plans to go back to my place in Jersey City. I was right where I wanted to be, with the people I wanted to be with.

THURSDAY, SEPTEMBER 13, 2001: "MAYBE SHE WAS THERE TO SAVE US"

My mother heard reports about the smoke at ground zero and that harmful elements might have been in it. She made an appointment for me to see a local doctor. He checked me out and said I was OK. He also told me that he was a trained psychologist. "How's the head," he asked. I said I was fine, perhaps a little on edge. He prescribed Valium. I took it.

The truth was my sleep had been fitful the night before. I didn't dream about 9/11, but my dreams were of struggle. Not happy dreams. They were dark and desperate. Since 9/11, those are the only kinds of dreams I've had. I no longer have any good dreams, the kinds from which you wake up and beautiful things have happened, or the kinds that make you feel like you're ready to go at life. I don't have those dreams anymore, not since ten years ago.

Media were calling from far and wide. John, the woman in the wheelchair, and I had become a national story.

John's parents drove up from North Carolina to take him home. They picked him up in Manhattan, then drove to my family's house in Verona. John, his parents, his aunt, and his sister sat down with my family for coffee in the kitchen. John and I left them to talk. We took a walk out to the backyard and sat down on a bench. John said, "It's crazy how much the media wants to speak with us since the *USA Today* article came out yesterday." I agreed. "You know, Mike," he said, "I can't help but feel weird, like undeserving." I knew what he meant. We didn't even know if the woman we carried was alive. Nobody knew. We just knew we carried her down. We knew we left her in an ambulance facing south. South was the wrong direction to go if you wanted to remain alive in the five minutes that followed our placing her in the ambulance. How likely was it that the ambulance made an immediate U-turn and got out of there? Based on my last memory of her, I believed she perished in the collapse of the North Tower.

I thought about what to say to John. I wanted to say something positive. I wanted to find some meaning in all of this. "Maybe she was there to save us," I said. "You see, even though we were there for almost the entire 102 minutes—from the time the first plane struck to the time the second tower went down— we managed to stay out of harm's way. We're not dead. We're not hurt. Maybe if we had gotten out at a different point in time, we would have been hit by flying debris. Or we would've stepped right into the fall of the South Tower. Or if we were just on our own, not carrying her, we would have taken a different turn—a wrong turn. But because of the timing of it all, because we moved at a certain speed by carrying that woman, we're still here."

"Well, maybe that's it," he said. "Did you even know her name?"

"No." I paused. "I never asked her."

John and his family left in the evening to stay with some friends in Fairfield, New Jersey. They would be heading home to North Carolina a day or two later.

Angelo returned home that night. He had been setting up a new optician's office in Watertown, New York, near the Canadian border. He and one of his bosses heard me on the CBC radio up there. He was the only member of my family I hadn't seen. It was very emotional. He gave me a big hug and gave me that look that said, *You don't know what you put us through.* Though we had talked on the phone a lot already, he was beside himself working in Upstate New York those past three days. He couldn't wait to get home. It was great to see my brother, to sit at his kitchen table and talk. We talked late into the night.

FRIDAY, SEPTEMBER 14, 2001

Network Plus wanted to see everybody. They organized a meeting of the World Trade Center office employees at their office in Newark, New Jersey. That's right. I still had a job.

I shot back to my apartment in Jersey City to pick up some clothes. I hadn't been there since the morning of 9/11. I understand better now why I didn't want to go back there. I wasn't ready to get back to any normalcy until I had made some sense of what had happened. I didn't want to get clothes, check the mail, or do anything like that. That life wasn't important to me anymore. Being trapped under that truck when the North Tower imploded—unable to breathe and unsure of whether I would make it—gave me a new perspective. It reduced things. Under that truck, I measured my life by what I would have lost if I didn't make it out. The answer was simple: the human connection to the people I loved. All I wanted to know was whether they were all right and to let them know I was all right. No other worldly concerns mattered. I just wanted to see my family. My reconnection with them allowed me to reconnect with the rest of the world.

But joining the "real world" again wasn't easy. Even Joy felt my resistance. I didn't realize it then, but I acted edgy and distant. I was just trying to keep it together in those first few days. I was desperately trying to regain control. I wanted no more surprises. No more trauma. I'd had enough of that.

In a strange way, 9/11 felt like a Friday to me, and Wednesday and Thursday were part of an extended weekend. Years of conditioning—working 7:30 a.m. to 6:30 p.m.—told me it was time to get back to work. When Network Plus called about a Friday meeting, it hit me like a ton of bricks that for so long, work had consumed me. Work was where I had spent most of the hours of my life. The last few days were a massive interruption of that routine. Since that "interruption," ten years ago, it has been incredibly difficult for me to return comfortably to a sustained "work" routine of any kind. It no longer occupies that same place of importance in my life. In fact, in most all aspects of my life, I see very little in the way I once did.

Before 9/11, I didn't know what it was like to witness a murder. I didn't know what it felt like to have one of the world's tallest buildings implode just feet from me. You might watch footage of 9/11 today and say to yourself, *I can't even imagine it. I don't know who I would be in that situation. Would I be able to function?* I was there, going through it, but I didn't even know what *it* was. I wasn't thinking about the size of devastation or how close I was to it, or the magnitude of the event itself. I was simply running from an exploding building. I was diving under a truck. I was *reacting*. And I think anyone would do that. I don't see myself as having done anything extraordinary. The week after 9/11, I snuck back to what they were calling Ground Zero. I took a good, long look at all the devastation. I saw massive pieces of twisted metal and fires and a ton of wreckage. *I came out of that! This fragile human flesh, skin, and bones came away without a mark!* Many other people suffered the complete opposite result. I continue to struggle with that fact, with the randomness of it all.

And what about that whole feeling of invincibility I walked into the office with on 9/11? I'd carried that feeling around for years before that day. I'd always possessed a self-generated confidence that my physical and mental ability could get me over and out of anything. I clung to that feeling as we moved through the North Tower. That mind-set got me through it. I never let the reality set in, never paused to think about how bad the situation was. The singular thought in my head while I was going down those stairs was, *No matter what comes up, find a way to get out of it.* Two basic forces propelled me forward: an unfounded sense of invincibility naturally coupled with an innate survival instinct. Where does one end and the other begin? I don't know. But I'm sure there were hundreds of people who were of the same mind-set, reacting the same way—reacting, reacting, reacting—until they reached that moment, that point where they knew they were going to die. They faced death. And to know that just kills me. That's the guilt I carry now. I had a brief moment of facing my own end. It was nothing, I'm sure, compared to what some people were going through—trapped, crushed, or taken by fire.

Watch videotapes of the plane hitting Tower 1 around the 93rd floor. I was twelve floors below that on the 81st floor. Watch tapes of the South Tower going down. I was right next door, somewhere between the 10th and 5th floors when it happened. Then watch tapes of the North Tower going down. I was running from that collapsing tower. Many other people did this. I wasn't the only one. Some people didn't make it, and we still don't know what happened to them. I can't stop thinking about other catastrophes: Pearl Harbor, Oklahoma City, the tsunami in Asia. I watch tapes of these events. I see real people. They are running. Some of them make it. Some of them don't. The only questions are, why did he make it, and why did she not make it? They're unanswerable.

* * *

Though the events of the previous few days gave me what you might call a new perspective on my professional career, getting back to work wasn't a bad idea. I thought it would be useful to get back in the swing of things and try to return to normalcy. Plus, it put my mind on something else. If I sat around and thought too much about what had happened, it became too overwhelming. Returning to work helped me signal to myself that I was OK. I was getting right back at it. There was a bit of a defiance to it as well. *You can knock me down, but you're not going to keep me down.* Going back to work was what I saw as the third step in the process of my self-restoration. Step 1: I'm OK. Step 2: My family is OK. Step 3: I'm back in life, engaged and participating.

The meeting at the Network Plus corporate office in Newark commenced at 10:00 a.m. on Friday. They brought in special trauma therapists. "Traumatists," I called them. It was probably a requirement of our health plan. Everyone who was inside the New York office when the plane struck was there, plus the people who had been out on calls, plus the entire Jersey office. It was a delicate atmosphere. We all walked on eggshells, making sure to be sensitive to what anyone might be going through. Via telephone contact over the last few days, I knew everyone had made it out safely. Some people sustained injuries, but nobody was hurt badly.

Our CEO and our VP of sales drove down from Massachusetts. Breakfast was catered in. People exchanged hugs and stories. We looked at each other, eye to eye, with a sincerity that did not exist before. They herded us into a separate room with the traumatists. We were encouraged, only if completely comfortable, to tell our stories. I looked around at my officemates. We had shared so much work and play. Now we shared this.

Mike Wright wasn't there because he was getting out of the hospital after suffering facial injuries when he got caught near the collapse of the South Tower. Kevin Nichols, Marc Reinstein, Jim Gaffney—they were there. Salespeople who were out of the office on calls that morning—they were there. John was there with his parents. From that meeting, he was heading straight back home with them to North Carolina. It was his last day.

The room was packed. Emotions were brimming at the surface. And the stories came out. Sujo John stood up to tell his story. I'll never forget it. His experience was purely from a religious perspective, his faith in God and calling out to Jesus. He spoke with a dazzling, dramatic flair. He told of how he was in a collapsed part of the building, in a hallway, in the dark with a group of people who somehow got separated from the others. He asked each person if they were ready to die, and if they were, were they ready to accept Jesus and yell his name "Jesus, Jesus, Jesus!" And the people began to yell the name. There were dead bodies around them. But all of a sudden, they began to see this light, which led them out of the building and into safety. He told this magnificent, emotional, spiritual story, and I was rapt. Some people didn't appreciate it at all. They felt that he was preaching. I didn't care. That was his story, and that's the way he felt.

I was hungry for everyone's story. They were all amazing to me. When it was my turn, people crowed, "Oh, we know your story." Somebody shouted with good-natured teasing, "Hero!" But I really didn't want to talk. I still held on to a little bit of that "I'm their manager" machismo. I wanted to hear everyone else's experiences and what they had gone through. There were some harrowing and tragic stories. Eric Martin was standing outside having a smoke when our building got hit. He moved out of the way at the last minute but saw someone impaled by huge shards of glass. It was an image that was hard for him to overcome. Some people got to the bottom of the World Trade Center mezzanine level after the second plane had hit and before the South Tower collapsed and saw unspeakable carnage out on the area where the globe and the fountain were. Neil Lucente and Peter Doran were riding an elevator when the tower was hit. The elevator shaft filled with flames, and they managed to jump from the car at the last second before it went sailing down. I wish I had a tape recorder for that session. These guys—many in their twenties, fresh out college—came together as a group and made it to safety because they looked out for each other. I was proud of them. This was my team. This was my office. They were all there, and they made it through this thing because they took care of each other. How are *they* not heroes?

I didn't want to go into my story. Like John and I discussed the day before, we felt guilty. *All of a sudden I'm a hero? How am I a hero if I don't even know whether or not I saved someone? I know I carried her down and put her in an ambulance, but I didn't even know if she was alive.* I was full of mixed emotions. *Yeah, I tried to do a good thing, but she might be dead!* Everyone knew my story from *USA Today,* but the story didn't mention whether she was alive or not. We didn't know. So we felt some embarrassment. It was weird. You have all this attention on you, and everybody is saying you did this heroic thing, and you have no idea whether the person you "saved" is alive.

The therapy session ended. We all filled out some paperwork and left early. It was a short day. Afterward, a bunch of us went over to the bar at the Newark Hilton. We ate some late lunch and had some drinks. We kept telling each other stories. We laughed a lot and took pictures. At some point, it came time for me to go. Dinner at my parents' house was waiting. We finally had the whole family together. I said good-bye to everyone and went to get my car, which was parked in the underground garage.

I called my mom from the garage to let her know I was running late. When I got off the phone with my mother, the phone rang. It was Lisa Kay Greissinger from *People* magazine. *OK, here we go again.* She started with "I'd like to commend you on the brave and heroic act you did. I think it was the greatest thing." I half-listened while fumbling for my car keys. "Tina Hansen is fine, and she told me—"

"What?" I said.

"Yes, Tina said that—"

"Who? *Who* did you say?"

"*Tina Hansen.* The way I got your number is because my husband is friends with Tina. Tina Hansen? The woman whom you carried down in the wheelchair? You gave her your card. That's how I got your name."

"She's alive?"

"Yes. I'm sorry. I . . . you didn't know? I'm sorry. I can call you back."

I hung up the phone. My throat began to tighten. Then my whole face pushed forward, and I burst out crying. I sat down in that parking garage and cried like a baby. All the sadness, the fear, the guilt—all of it—came to a head and came pouring out of me. I got so excited I ran back into the bar with tears in my eyes. It had already been an emotional day. My gang had had a few drinks by now. Somebody joked, "Oh, what's he crying about?" I told them, and they bought me a drink. I called home and told them. I called John, and we shouted together like teammates who had just won the big game. Much of our rejoicing came from the relief of finally knowing that what we did—what the newspapers were saying we did—now meant so much more to us. We were, on a very powerful, personal level, liberated.

The *People* magazine reporter called back a little later and asked if she could arrange a photo shoot for the magazine. How about Monday? She asked. Sure. We hung up. The phone rang again. It was Tina. I spoke to her. "I didn't know if you were alive. I didn't know your name. I remember giving you the card . . ." I can barely remember the conversation. I was so overcome with joy. Tina was matter-of-fact. She'd had this handicap since she was three, so she was no stranger to struggle. She was very independent, very strong-willed. "I didn't know you didn't know," she said. "Thank you, Michael. I guess I'll see you on Monday." We hung up. That was the highest point. In the midst of so much pain and trauma and confusion, I felt some measure of redemption. For a moment the world seemed to come back to me. I had seen my friends from work. I was heading home to be with my family. And I knew, finally, that her name was Tina, and she was alive.

PART IV

A HERO'S WELCOME?

SEPTEMBER 2001–SEPTEMBER 2002

"Hey Mike, did President Bush call you today?"

Angelo and I are the type of brothers who like to bust each other's chops. That's our rhythm. Having heard just a couple hours earlier that the woman in the wheelchair, Tina Hansen, was alive, and then promptly spilling my emotional guts all over the Newark Hilton parking garage, some levity across the dinner table from Angelo was all right with me.

"Very funny, Anj." I smirked at him and then kissed my mom on the cheek.

But Angelo wasn't joking.

"No, seriously," said Angelo. "He talked about you. Well, not you *per se*. But today, in his speech, he mentioned what you did."

I looked at my father. He nodded his head, gently saying without words, *Your brother's not kidding.*

The phone had been ringing all day. Actually, it had been ringing nonstop for four days straight since the moment I got reception back, walking uptown and out of the wreckage on 9/11. I couldn't keep up. I didn't want to keep up. I was all talked out about 9/11. No more interviews please. Not from media, family, friends—anybody. I started deleting messages from numbers I didn't know.

Could I have deleted *the president?*

After dinner I sat on the couch with my parents and Joy and watched a replay of President Bush's address from the National Cathedral on what was being called a National Day of Prayer and Remembrance. And sure enough, he said it. President George W. Bush said,

> And we have seen our national character in eloquent acts of sacrifice: Inside the World Trade Center, one man who could have saved himself stayed until the end and at the side of his quadriplegic friend. A beloved priest died giving the last rites to a firefighter. *Two office workers, finding a disabled stranger, carried her down 68 floors to safety.* A group of men drove through the night from Dallas to Washington to bring skin grafts for burned victims. In these acts and many others, Americans showed a deep commitment to one another and an abiding love for our country.

I looked at Joy. I looked at my parents. This was all too much. First I find out about Tina Hansen. *People* magazine wanted to take our picture on Monday. Now this? Now the *president of the United States?*

I can't tell you it wasn't an amazing thing. It was. But it was overwhelming. The totality of the events of that day and night pummeled me into a state of vertigo. None of it seemed real. I couldn't feel myself anymore. Was I happy, embarrassed, fearful, grateful?

Don't feel a thing. Not one thing. You let in one feeling, you let them all in.

I just wanted to lie down, go to sleep, and have my life back. I wanted it to be over. Maybe if I closed my eyes, something would show me the way out in the morning. Maybe there would be answers.

People arranged to do the photo shoot with Tina at her apartment on the Lower East Side on Monday afternoon, September 17. Coincidentally, Network Plus arranged to move us to another one of their office locations in Manhattan, the Starrett-Lehigh Building on West 26th Street, that same day.

I walked into the new office first thing Monday morning, ready to work, the first one in the office. I figured that was better than staying at home and thinking about everything. Well, I didn't consciously figure it that way. Unconsciously, I was trying not to fully accept, or even acknowledge, all that had happened. *The best way to handle this is to get back to work, prove that we were knocked down but now we're back up.* A truer statement of my state of mind would've been, *I can fake it, distract myself, fool myself, act like I don't feel the things I feel, and going to work is one way to do that.*

I took a tally of who was there and who was not. Many were not there. My people were not ready to come back yet. No one was being forced to come back immediately. John had gone back to North Carolina. So there was at least one salesperson who wouldn't be returning.

And with John not physically in New York, I became the point of focus for the media. It seemed like everybody had my phone number. They asked for both of us, and after a while, they started asking only for me. Maybe it was because of the story—I managed the office, I found Tina, I put things in motion on the 68th floor. But let's be clear. If it wasn't for John, neither Tina nor I might be here.

As boxes were being unpacked, I left the office in the hands of electricians and IT people and ran downtown for the photo shoot.

I was nervous. Being in *People* magazine, doing a photo shoot—this was weird for me. Also, heading in a downtown direction made me queasy. Walking around Manhattan, less than a week after the attacks, you felt it—the lack of a basic sense of security. The wound was still fresh. We were just getting off the mat. It was in the air, and the tension got thicker as you moved nearer in the direction of what they were calling Ground Zero.

Most of all, this would be the first time I'd see Tina since closing those ambulance doors.

I got there on time and knocked on the apartment door, which was slightly ajar. Voices carried into the hallway. A *People* staffer pulled the door open while I was in mid-knock. My eyes darted through several other unfamiliar bodies until they rested on Tina. I wanted to see *her*. That whole day carrying her down, I was just carrying a body, some *person*. I didn't get to know her at all. I didn't know her name. In the last four days, I had gone from not knowing if she was alive to learning that she was, and now seeing her.

This is a happy thing. This is something I can feel good about.

We talked a little. I was cautious. I wasn't comfortable with how much I should mention. I sensed caution in her too. But we needed to know things. We had questions for each other: What do you remember? Do you remember when this happened? Did you see that? How did you get out? I wanted to go back over it in my head to make sure I had things right—if my experience matched hers. She told me the ambulance took right off. Had it not, she would not be here. With that, we broke eye contact and looked down. There were prolonged silences between us, but neither of us seemed to mind. We stayed close to each other in the room. She asked what happened to me. Did she see the footage of me running? Had she heard other survival stories? There was so much I wanted to talk about, but there was too little time and too many people in the room.

It was all so sudden. 9/11 was Tuesday. Less than a week later, Monday, 9/17, I'm in her apartment doing a photo shoot. I found it difficult to fully take it all in. I figured the only reason I was in there was because Tina worked with the husband of Lisa Kay Greissinger, who worked for *People*, who contacted me. That's the way things happen sometimes. I didn't think of myself as anything special, as a national hero. I saw myself as disoriented, grasping for anything that offered clarity and balance. And other than John, Tina was my only other human link to what went on inside those stairwells. She was the one person, I thought, who could really understand me. Everyone else, to me, required an unloading—a wrenching, painfully long explanation. Tina just knew. It felt good to be around her.

When it came time to finally pose for the shoot, both of us felt strange. *What are we posing for anyway?* The people from *People* were very kind, gently imparting instructions while the photographer clicked away. I guess we seemed stiff. Finally, the photographer pulled his face back from behind the camera and broke through the seriousness: "Just give her a hug!" I reached over and clutched Tina, and a huge smile broke out across my face. That's the picture they used.

They wrapped the shoot. I had to get back to work. Tina and I exchanged phone numbers and e-mail addresses. I left her apartment, good-byes all around. And that was the second time I met Tina Hansen.

In the year to follow, Tina and I would do a lot more media together. We had a full 9/11 reunion when John came into town some weeks after the *People* shoot, and we all went to lunch. Tina was never comfortable with the media attention. She had once even said, "Try not to mention me when they interview you." It was suggested to me that perhaps her reticence had to do with her working for the Port Authority. The fact that she was on the 68th floor and it took someone from the 81st floor to carry her out might not have looked too good for her employer. Tina was always gracious and grateful with the media, but could not fully indulge in the idea of celebrating our story. The way I see it, she is a woman who had sustained a dignified battle with rheumatoid arthritis since age three. She worked daily to eliminate dependence. In our story, on 9/11, she was the very thing she'd spent her whole life trying not to be: a victim. Why would she want to celebrate her victimhood?

As the newspapers continued to count the "victims" of 9/11, I found it near impossible to celebrate anything, even being alive.

I can't go there. I can't get stuck in feelings like that.

As if I was still trying to get down the stairs in the North Tower, the voice in my head directed me to shut down any thoughts that hurt, or could hurt—thoughts that could hurtle me backward.

The best thing for me to do was go back to the office, dive back into work, dive back into life. Start forgetting about 9/11. But 9/11 wouldn't let me. The office phone, my cell phone, my parents' phone wouldn't stop ringing. *The Today Show, Good Morning America, The Early Show*—every show, every magazine, every reporter, writer, and producer wanted to talk to me. I wasn't answering. I had an office to put back together. *No, thank you.*

Before 9/11, I had forty-five people working in our World Trade Center North Tower office. Twenty-eight of them were in the office on 9/11. Now it became my job to get everyone who went through the experience back to work. We had begun to hire many of our people straight out of college. They were young. Now they were scared. They were not coming in. If they did, it would be for a day or an hour, and then they'd go home "sick." Some were taking prescription Valium and other sedatives. Some were drinking heavily. I guess we all were drinking more heavily. I noticed many were losing sleep. People were having a hard time dealing with it. A couple of reps decided they could no longer be in the city. I understood. So I devised a plan.

I called each one of them in the morning and said, "Look, I don't care if you stay at work. You just come down here, see me, and if you want to go back home, go back home. But all I want you to do is get up and come see me in this office. After that, the day is yours." Eventually, I got everyone to come back to work full-time.

By October, I had a sales force again. We had a good October too. New York City was a nerve-racking place in those first days and weeks after 9/11. I remember going out to have a smoke, hearing sirens, and getting an uneasy feeling, thinking, *Is it terrorism?* Then they said anthrax was traveling through the mail. Then a plane went down in Rockaway Beach.

Life pre- and post-9/11 were entirely different in every way.

My pre-9/11 Network Plus mind-set was all about the public offering, the stock value, growing the company. My post-9/11 mind-set on Network Plus? I had little concern with long-term business goals. I was going day by day. Get up. Go to work. Get through the day. My drug of choice was bravado. Bravado can keep you from facing yourself in a lot of ways.

But there was another pre-9/11 preoccupation I had more trouble navigating. Pre-9/11, I had just gotten engaged. The morning of 9/11, wedding plans dominated my life. Two weeks before 9/11, we booked the place where we were going to get married. Now the wedding barely registered for me. It was secondary. How unfair to Joy. Not only was the wedding no longer the biggest thing in our lives, but I wasn't the same. Pre-9/11, all we talked about was the wedding, the fun things we would do that day, our lives together. Post-9/11, she's dealing

with my distracted and haphazard "Oh, right . . . the wedding."
She's engaged to a guy who is no longer emotionally or psychologically available. She looks over at her fiancé and sees a person
in a state of shock. She doesn't see the same guy she planned
to marry. When you watch tapes of my television appearances,
you can see it in my eyes. I'm just not there. That's what Joy
always said. She could tell that night—the night of 9/11—the
moment we first and finally saw each other. I just wasn't there.
I was gone.

That was the hardest thing. I wasn't there because I didn't
want to accept a lot of things. I was afraid. I was afraid to delve
into the effect those things had on me—the things I saw, what
I went through. My pre-9/11 personality for dealing with life's
little adversities was to handle *it*, put *it* aside, and move on.
But this thing—9/11—could not simply be put aside. You can't
move on from *it* without facing *it*, fully. To be my old self, I'd
have to eat *it* up, chew *it* up, re-taste *it*, and re-digest *it*—all of *it*
and what *it* really was to me. Deep down, I knew that's what it
would take. There was no way I could do *it*.

I look back now, and I can see myself in those early days. Joy
wanted to discuss the wedding, but I was no help. I sat there,
physically present in conversations—in our kitchen or in our
living room or at a Home Depot—talking about it, but not
present. My mouth was moving, and words were coming out,
but I wasn't feeling it. I'd respond with dismissive brevity. "Yeah,
sure, OK. You take care of it."

In those days, it was also not lost on either of us that the date
of our wedding—September 13, 2002—was right around the
one-year anniversary of 9/11. The intertwining of those events
was inescapable. *Is this a message?* we'd ask ourselves. *Should we
save the money and just run off to Vegas?* We seriously considered
it. I said we might regret it. I think Joy knew better but didn't

say it. We stuck to our plan. We'd get married two days after the first anniversary of 9/11.

"You sure this is the right thing for us?" she asked me. The phone rang again. This time I picked it up. *A call from the media should require less real feelings than talking about the wedding.* This is how I was operating.

Friday, September 21, 2001

I got through my first full week in the new office.

On Friday night, September 21, I'm sitting on the couch with Joy at my parents' house. We're watching TV. I'm tense, mind racing, saying little. We flip through channels, but every network is showing this huge, live telethon called *America: A Tribute to Heroes.* The event was raising money for victims and families of victims of 9/11. In America, the telethon was simulcast by over thirty-five network and cable channels, broadcast on over eight thousand radio stations, and streaming on the Internet. You couldn't turn on any device you owned without seeing or hearing it.

My phone rings again. It's the people from the telethon. They don't want money. They want permission to use my name. I didn't know what they were asking, exactly. Did they want to mention it when they called people for donations? Did they think *I* needed money? But yeah, sure, OK, I said.

Joy and I were enjoying the show. Various celebrities came on, one after the other, telling about different poignant and powerful things that happened on the day, and then a song was performed after the telling of each inspiring story. I was gripped by it. I felt connected to every story they told. It was really beautifully done. Then Jim Carrey came on. He told *my story.* He said my name and John Cerqueira's name. He spoke about selflessness and being a hero and acts of kindness, how we put our lives at risk to save someone else. Enrique Iglesias followed him and sang "Hero."

I was blown away. This was different from *USA Today* or the CBS news footage, which to me was all about news reporting. This wasn't *People* magazine, where the writer knew Tina Hansen's husband. This was ten days later. To be singled out on this kind of show, running on every network—I mean, the words "Oh my god" flew out of my mouth.

That elevated things. It became clear to me that our story was circulating in the national oxygen. It started to sink in. First, President Bush, and now this. *My story* was positive. It carried a positive message that we—the country, the victims, the survivors—could all be proud of. I sat there on the couch with my fiancée and my parents, and *I* felt *proud* of it. *This is who we really are. That's what I really saw in the Tower and on the ground.* That worked for me. It released a good feeling in me.

You see, as much as everyone was patting me on the back, I was not having too many good feelings on Friday, September 21, 2001. I was having nightmares. I said nothing about it to anyone, but underneath my stony silence, I was shaky. Hearing the president refer to me seven days after 9/11, and then being singled out during a national telethon three days after that gave me hope. I had no answers, but those two things pushed open a door, letting in some daylight of belief in me that maybe there was some meaning to what I went through. Amid all the twisted and fucked-up feelings, this feeling was OK. *If the White House and the producers of a nationally broadcast telethon feel good about it, maybe I should feel good about it too. Feel good instead of feel anger and sorrow and guilt.* Those two things let me feel that I did something right, instead of feeling that I did something wrong. Friends called me that night, saying, "Hey, did I just hear Jim Carrey say your name?" I said, "Yeah. I can't believe it."

I *smiled.* That show gave me permission to smile. It made me want to personally thank Jim Carrey for my first truly solid good feeling in ten days.

Maybe I'm really OK. Maybe it's OK to talk about this publicly, with other people.

Up until that moment, I couldn't hold one good thought in my head. I looked at others, and they always seemed to know something I didn't. On 9/12, after my CEO, Rob Hale, saw the CBS feed and led the *USA Today* reporter to me, he said, "Mike, you've got to understand—you're a national hero." I was like, "What are you talking about? I'm still trying to figure shit out. I don't even know if she's alive. I'm checking to see if I still have my nuts attached. I'm making sure I didn't lose anybody from our office. Man, I was choking to death with my face against the pavement and my ass in the air, halfway under a goddamn truck. I'm just pulling my head together. I saw *bodies* coming down from the sky. The firemen. The firemen. The firemen!" But nobody wants to know that. The TV's on, didn't you know? I'm standing amid death, dust, and rubble; I've just witnessed horrors unimaginable; and all of a sudden, a camera is in my face. And I spew out what happened. I had no idea, nor did I care that it was being fed by CBS to the world. And because of that, the next conversation that afternoon, maybe two hours later, is with my CEO, who says, "You are a national hero." *What?* That made absolutely no sense to me. I just saw a person and then another person jump—*fucking jump*—from the top of the World Trade Center. That's why maybe the only purely true thing I said to that CBS cameraman was "This is chaos," refer-ring to everything, *including the camera people documenting the chaos.* Hero of fucking what? Madness, that's what.

I guess that's how things happen. I told a CBS cameraman that I had just carried a woman down sixty-eight floors, not realizing that I was in the middle of some national media moment. If that cameraman had walked ten feet to the left, he'd have met a woman who saved somebody else. Ten feet to the right, he'd have met a man who made sure his friend stopped crying so they could walk the last ten floors. I just happened to be standing where someone needed me. That's all. But national hero? Say those words, and *boom*, people are on it. They're on me. The media buzz is instant, immediate. And ten days later, I've got to navigate it?

The president and a nationwide emergency telethon recognized me on national television. What do I do about this? Do I have a responsibility of some kind? Should I be doing more? Should I be doing less? You try to wrap your head around it. People are saying you should get an agent. I'm getting offers sent to me from Hollywood for "my story." I'm getting offers to speak at all kinds of public functions. It's crazy. I still have a full-time job with Network Plus. Yet I'm starting to see it. After the president and the telethon, I am coming to believe that people can take something good from what happened that day. They need to. Because there was good to take. All my reps made it. Tina made it. Yet how do you appropriately express that good? There were too many people who didn't make it, too many people in mourning. So much pain everywhere. You couldn't help but feel that by talking about the good that happened— about surviving—that you were doing something wrong.

But all those phone calls I had been ignoring, they weren't going to end. President Bush and Jim Carrey saw to that. They also got me believing that maybe I could help others.

I should pick up the phone.

So I said yes to *Good Morning America*. Was I thinking *I'm a hero*? No. But If I could tell my story and maybe somebody somewhere would feel better, then I'd do it. I was very conflicted about it. The nation was in mourning. I was in mourning. The nation was hurting. I was hurting. And I was nervous as hell.

Tuesday, September 25, 2001

Charlie Gibson was a cool guy. A guy's guy. He made John and me feel calm. He was professional and sensitive. He saw we were TV rookies, and he explained to us how things would go. He said, "Just talk to me like we're buddies on the street." And that's exactly how he conducted things when the cameras started to roll. *This feels wrong. My mouth is moving, but I feel like I'm in somebody else's skin.* I was feeling that alien feeling I had in the bar the night of 9/11.

The interview was short. They ask questions. You answer questions. And that's the story you tell. But in my head, it was, *Yes, I carried this woman down, but just after that, I ran from this exploding building, man. I heard the thing explode behind me. I ran for my life.* I understood the woman-in-the-wheelchair story was what they wanted. But what I wanted someone to know was that three minutes after I put her in an ambulance, I was really close to dying in an atmosphere of overwhelming terror. I never felt that I was ever really getting across what happened that day and how I felt. Carrying Tina out was a great thing. She made it. But what raged in my memory was seeing the firemen, the bodies, the things that happened *after* I got out of the building. That's what consumed me. What the hell was I going to say about that? I couldn't bring up the horror, could I? I was angry. I just wanted to scream into the camera. I wanted to tell everyone who lost something that I felt them. *I feel your loss. I feel your loss. I feel your loss.*

When I got into the office that morning, I took a good ribbing from everybody. My family and Joy saw the show too. But all they saw was the distance in my eyes. They were thinking,

What's wrong with him? Maybe he should be concentrating more on himself. Should he really be doing this?

That was the paradox. I get kudos on national TV, but my family can see I'm not healthy. Wherever I go they're calling me a hero and clapping their hands, but the nation is in mourning, crying. They show my face on television and in magazines, and I walk outside to see thousands of faces of the missing on photographs posted everywhere.

"Great job this morning, Mike," my CEO told me over the phone. "Now, up next, I really want to make sure you're fully on board for this *Oprah* thing."

"I am, Rob," I reassured him. And then I asked again, "But seriously, is she really *that* popular?"

OPRAH

I didn't know Oprah Winfrey was that big of a deal. It just wasn't something I was aware of. Calls from the media came into our office all the time. I hung up on so many producers. Some calls I just didn't take at all. A producer from *The Oprah Winfrey Show* had called every day since 9/12 asking me to be on the show. He called me, and he called our home office in Massachusetts trying to get to me. I wasn't interested. The producers were shocked that I wouldn't do it, that I didn't scream into the telephone like a schoolgirl. I guess they didn't hear "no" too often. Plus, their approach wasn't entirely sensitive. It was all business. They were abrupt. And I get it. They've got a job to do. They're trying to put a show together. I didn't expect them to be my therapist. I just had no interest in selling my story like it was processed food. Plus, to go all the way out to Chicago didn't sound like a good use of my time.

They put another producer on it. Let's call him Roy. His approach was not much different than that of the other producers. He got to my CEO, who urged me to take the call. Roy said he wanted to do a "survivor story."

"I don't know, Roy," I said. "I'm really not sure this is for me."

He wasn't listening. "Now, Michael," he said, "I need you to send in personal photos, write up a short summary . . ." E-mail this, fax that, make a list of this . . . He just kept going. I looked incredulously at the phone in my hand. Finally, I got a little irritated. "You want to do a survivor's story, Roy? I've got forty survivors outside my office door. You want me to be on the show? Get them on the show." There was a pause on the other line. Roy spoke: "Maybe that can be arranged," he said. Then he said he'd call me right back.

I had been feeling guilty about all the attention focused on me. *Damn it, my guys were survivors. They were on the 81st floor, and every one of them made it out. They all have stories. They're all hurting. They all experienced horrific things and did amazing things, and nobody's calling them. I'm not the only survivor.*

Roy called back. He actually called my CEO, Rob Hale. The next thing you know, we're all going out to Chicago to be on *The Oprah Winfrey Show,* Thursday, September 27. John and I would be on the couch with Oprah. The rest of the office would be in the audience. A couple guys in the office would be featured from their seats. Oprah paid for my ticket, John's ticket, and my CEO's ticket. My CEO bought flights for all the reps.

I had three simple objectives/conditions for this trip:

1. I wanted to get my guys out of New York and have a night on the town together, as an office, in Chicago before the show. But they wanted to fly us out late Wednesday night before the 9:00 a.m. Thursday CT taping, and put us back on a plane right

after the show. I said no way. I made them change the plans so we could fly out Wednesday morning and have a day together in Chicago. After we made the final flight arrangements, I heard from Oprah's staff that she got wind of our plan to be there the day before. You know what Oprah did? In addition to putting us all up on her dime at the Omni Chicago Hotel, she gave each one of us $100 per diem to spend at the hotel. Her generosity left me speechless. What class. So my first objective was achieved by the grace of Oprah Winfrey.

2. I wanted to make sure I mentioned the name of our regional manager, Kevin Nichols, on air. Though I had started the process, Kevin was really instrumental in organizing everyone to go down the stairwells while I stayed behind to check the bathrooms and elevators.

3. I wanted to thank, on air, Mrs. Toussaint's fifth-grade class from Heights Elementary School in Sharon, Massachusetts. Those kids sent me postcards that kept me glued together at a time when I was, minute by minute, nearly falling apart. I still have every one of those cards, and they still heal me when I hold them.

I came home after work one night, during that first mind-blurring week after 9/11. I was exhausted from sleepless nights—stomach knotted, nerves jangled, phone ringing—and there among a pile of mail was this manila envelope with twenty crayoned cards in it. The kids drew pictures of me. One had me in a Superman costume. One had me standing on the Towers. One depicted a man carrying a woman in a building with flames coming out of it. I sat down, held these cards in my hands, and I felt . . . *stillness.*

I did not know it then, but what was to come, starting with Oprah, was a journey of nonstop formal public appearances and high-profile media engagements. And when those cards arrived, it was the beginning of the most consistently good feeling I had doing such things, and that feeling always had to do with kids. When kids were involved, it touched me in a way that let me be me again. Kids—like when I sat holding my nephew the day after 9/11 and I was able to feel my feelings, even though they were very difficult feelings to feel. Kids somehow defrosted me. I could not articulate it, but when kids were part of the plans, the noise in my head—the million discordant voices of guilt, anger, fear, grief, imbalance, loss—quieted, and I felt peace. And though my thoughts remained nearly impossible to articulate, among kids my mind seemed ordered, my perspective seemed sensible, my balance was temporarily restored instead of constantly careening from one unwanted feeling to another. After 9/11, the only time I found that equilibrium was with kids, and the first time after 9/11 I felt it was when I was holding those cards from Mrs. Toussaint's fifth-grade class.

I hold notes like these more dear than any national attention I received. There's so much honesty to them. I look at these cards, and they bring me back to when I was a kid doing something like that in class, filling my head with imaginings of what a grown-up person like the one I was thinking about felt like. These kids were trying to understand what was going on as their TVs at home played it back relentlessly. Then they hear about it from their teacher who knows "the guy." (Mrs. Angela Toussaint married Jeff Toussaint, my Theta Delta Chi fraternity brother and roommate my senior year at Brown.) They feel especially connected. I sat there holding those cards, man, thinking about those kids sitting at their desks, creating each one and addressing them to me. So creative, truthful, sensitive in saying "Thank you."

I wanted them to know how much that meant to me. I wanted to thank them on national television, on *The Oprah Winfrey Show*.

Truth is, by the time I went on *Oprah*, I had gotten so many e-mails and cards from so many people, every day. Cards from total strangers saying the kindest things. I wanted to show proper appreciation to every single one of them. I wanted to read a list of every name on the next national TV show I went on. There were just so, so many. Beautiful words, so caringly expressed to me about what I did and how it connected to them, whether because they had a child with a disability or loved someone in a wheelchair or someone with a debilitating disease, or they knew someone in the building, or they lost someone in the fire. These notes, which nobody but me alone saw or read, when nobody was looking, went straight to my core. These notes kept me going. If there was a medicine I was supposed to take in the early days just after, these notes were it. They also reinforced to me that maybe what I did shouldn't be kept quiet. Maybe it should be shared.

My reps got out to Chicago late Wednesday morning. The idea of flying was scary in those days. 9/11 was only two weeks prior. Consequently, a few of my reps didn't make the trip. The thought of flying was too nerve-racking for them. One of my reps backed out practically before boarding. That's how it was then.

I took a separate flight, which got me into Chicago in the late afternoon. A limo picked me up at O'Hare Airport. I made quick use of the limo bar. My gang was waiting for me at the hotel, and we headed out to paint the town red. We arrived at Tavern On Rush.

When a group of fortysome people pile into a bar, the rest of the place is like, *Who are these guys?* The Tavern On Rush manager found out that night exactly who we were and why we were there. And he rolled out the red carpet. It was more than I could've asked for. The manager cordoned off our own private section. Other patrons came in to talk to us. Every single one of my guys was being treated for a night like a national hero. Everybody was giving and getting hugs from Chicagoans we did not know who just wanted to show unity between Chicago and New York. On top of everything, my best friend, Jeff Fernandez, who was living in Indianapolis, drove in and met me there. It was my first time seeing him since 9/11 took place. I soaked in this dream night for every minute it lasted. Then I checked my watch, and it was 2:00 a.m. There was a limo coming at 7:00 a.m. to take me to Harpo Studios.

Roy met us in the production room at Harpo. Time to match names with faces. Roy greeted us by checking off who was who, taking attendance. "From Network Plus: Rob Hale, CEO, uh-huh. Mike Wright, uh-huh. Adam Andrews, uh-huh. John Cerqueira, uh-huh." And then he stops at me and sniffs. "Oh. Who's this? Mike Benfante?" Staring down his clipboard at me. "Oh yes, you're exactly how I pictured you." He clearly wasn't meaning it as a compliment. That's how Roy and I started off that morning.

I will say it now: Roy and I did not have the best relationship. Even before the day of the shoot, our dialogue was always challenging. I didn't think he was very sensitive to the whole situation, and he probably thought I didn't express the requisite gratitude for the opportunity. It takes two to tango, so I'll take responsibility for my part. But this is how I recall how that day went down:

As soon as we got into the greenroom, we had been given a bunch of releases to sign. I suppose I was being overcautious, but I didn't want to sign one of those releases. Rob Hale nudged me nervously. "Mike," he said, "what are you doing? C'mon, let's move this along." But I wouldn't do it. Then John wouldn't do it, either. They had to have a verbal agreement for me to show my image on TV. So John goes along with me down to a sound room, and we verbally record our assent. I'm becoming increasingly annoyed with Roy's treatment of us, and Roy can't believe my behavior. The tension is building. Roy comes out and lets us know how the show will proceed: First, the Rudy Giuliani segment. Then a segment on Flight 93 with Lisa Beamer, who lost her husband; Alice Hoagland, who lost her son; and the United Airlines air phone operator, Lisa D. Jefferson, who tried to comfort the passengers. Then us. Any questions? I raise my hand. "Yes, Roy," I say. "I have a question. I got these cards from fifth graders in Sharon, Massachusetts, and I'd just like to quickly thank them during the show." He bounces the index and middle fingers of his right hand against his pursed lips, feigning consideration. "Uhhhhh, I don't think so. We're pretty pressed for time. In fact, we're already behind. Besides, isn't this something you can just do over the phone?" I was livid. "Jesus, Roy! Screw you!"

"Mike!" shouted Rob Hale as he placed himself between me and Roy, like an ice hockey referee creating distance between brawlers. "You need to calm down."

I am going to thank those kids anyway.

I tucked the envelope with the cards under my arm. "OK, Roy," I said, flashing Roy the universal "OK" hand sign while reassuringly patting my CEO on the back. From then on, wherever I went, that envelope went with me.

Despite my tiff with Roy, I actually felt quite humbled to be in that greenroom. We were in tremendous company. Lisa Beamer, the woman whose husband, Todd, was credited with saying "Let's roll," was there, as was the United Airlines phone operator Lisa D. Jefferson, who handled calls from victims during the hijacking.

And then there was Alice Hoagland, the mother of Mark Bingham, a rugby player, who had fought back. She was so gracious, so considerate. She listened to *me*. Man, she was the one whom I was concerned about. But Alice Hoagland gave me a hug, and in doing so, the mother who lost her son made *me* feel good about being a survivor. I'll never forget her. How soon it was for her to go talk about this after losing her son. I could barely keep it together, and I was here, alive. I don't know where people get the strength, but they do. Alice Hoagland did. She was amazing to me.

We were minutes from showtime. My reps were out in the audience. Rob Hale went out to join them. The first segment, the Giuliani interview via satellite, began. The greenroom got a little quieter, with each guest exiting in succession for their segments, ultimately leaving just John and me. And I was getting more and more nervous.

Commercial break.

It was almost time for John and me to go on. A couple of girls walked us to the stage entrance. They were sweethearts. In fact, all of Oprah's staff, with the exception of Roy, were incredibly courteous, fun, and professional. The especially sweet production assistant escorting me noticed my envelope of precious cards tucked snugly under my arm.

"Oooh, and what do you have there?" she asked.

I softly told her what they were and what I would like to do. She nodded with such understanding and asked supportively, "Where will you keep them while you're onstage?"

I said, "I'll sit on them if I have to."

And with a big smile on her face, she said, "I'm sorry, but I'm going to have to take those. You can't go out there with them."

"Really?" I asked.

"Really."

I unclutched my arm and surrendered the envelope. As I am letting go, I read the front of it. "Heights Elementary School, Sharon Massachusetts, Mrs. Toussaint's fifth-grade class." And I repeated it to myself over and over again.

"THIRTY SECONDS TO AIR," barks some guy with a headset. I'm standing next to John. My head is about to explode. We got our cue and walked out onstage. The first thing I saw were my guys in the audience. Huge smiles were beaming from their faces. It was awesome. They were so excited to be there. We used to do this thing with each other in the office. It was like the fist bump, but we held it low, and there was no bump. So on my way to Oprah's couch, I gave them the low fist, and everybody cracked up. I did too.

They put young and handsome John next to Oprah and sat my grizzled visage on the outermost seat away from Oprah, to John's left. That was all right with me. The interview began, and I can barely remember a word of it. John seemed to do most of the talking. I sat pretty stoic, tight-faced. I was preoccupied with how to get the fifth graders mentioned.

Oprah was great. It's all true about her. She just makes you feel perfectly comfortable. The woman is effortlessly and naturally a person you'd just want to hang out with and talk to. What a pro. Immediate warmth. So down to earth.

We had not met her before that moment. I felt much better as soon as she began talking to us. At a point early in the interview, when I explained how we got everyone to the center of the office, I said, "And our regional manager, Kevin Nichols, had our administrative assistant by the arm." I checked that off my list. Two down, one to go.

We break for commercial. John and Oprah are yammering away. This might be my only shot. I lean over and break in, "Hey Oprah, I got these cards from some fifth graders in the mail. What do you think?"

She waved her hand munificently forward and said, "Oh sure, hon! That's a fantastic idea. Tell you what, when we come back from commercial, I'll cue you, and you do your thing. OK?" *Yes, Oprah. Now I'm OK.*

When they came back in from commercial, you could see how my face changed. I was happy, loose. We're back in, and Oprah says, "I'm sure you have received notes from well-wishers since this happened, Michael."

My face lit up. "Yes, Oprah, in particular . . ." I fit in everything, except I forgot Mrs. Toussaint's name. But I did it. I thanked those kids on TV. After that, I kicked back and enjoyed the show.

At the end, Oprah hugged us. I remember my cousin saying that Oprah must have liked me because when she hugged me, she lifted her foot up.

There is one part of the *Oprah* show that I wish I didn't have to mention, but I feel I must. Toward the end of our segment, Oprah went to the audience to interview a few of my reps. Mike Wright, for example, had a tremendous story about his staying behind to administer CPR and then getting caught in the collapse of Tower 2. Oprah also let another manager of mine, Adam Andrews, tell his story.

In the first moments right after the plane hit our building, after we got everyone out of the office, Adam was the last one to exit the office with me. We came down the stairwell together. Right around the time, or right after the time I ran into John, I lost track of Adam. Well, Adam proceeded to tell Oprah how he saved a number of people by preventing them from jumping out of windows. This didn't make sense to a lot of us. The problem is there were no windows broken at that level in the tower. There was no reason for anyone to jump below the 81st floor.

Perhaps he kept people calm and helped them down a stairwell, but as far as directly preventing people from jumping out a window, it didn't happen. As Oprah is interviewing him, you can see me wriggling in my seat and getting very uneasy with the whole thing. To me, and to others who were in Tower 1 on 9/11, his story was so obviously untrue. Yet he insisted on talking about it. I had never heard this story before that moment. When we got back to New York, the whole office felt uncomfortable.

Back in New York, I pulled him aside privately. "Just be careful about what you say and how you present yourself because you will be questioned about it," I said. I especially wanted to tell him this because we learned that he was scheduled to receive an award with John and me at the annual CompTel Conference and Trade Exposition in Boston in October. He told his story there, anyway. I felt very uncomfortable about it, but I also felt like, *Who am I to question him?* But there would be some who would question him. I knew that after the CompTel ceremony we were going to be interviewed by *The Wall Street Journal*, so I warned Adam one more time: "Listen," I said. "You are going to sit down with a journalist, and she is going to interview you about this incident. You have to be really careful about what you are going to say. And know that because I was not there with you, I am not going to be able to substantiate anything you say." Sure enough, we met with a *Wall Street Journal* reporter. She questioned him, all right. "Wait a minute," she said. "You're telling me you saved people, but there was no fire on the floors you are talking about. Why would anyone want to jump out a window?" And she's looking at me, and I'm looking straight down. I didn't talk to Adam much after that night. I don't know why he said what he said, but it was, well, sickening.

I had been so deliberate about managing my guilt. I had been so insistent about qualifying all my reps as heroes. I was so tortured from battling images of firefighters and jumpers. Right up to and during the moment I sat on Oprah Winfrey's couch, I picked and sorted, wallowed in, and then ignored all these feelings, still and always profoundly doubting whether I had any right to talk to anyone about anything. If I spoke in public, I wanted in the utmost, and if nothing else, to be sensitive to families in pain. And this guy gets on *Oprah* and flat-out lies? Why? For God's sakes, why? I've never mentioned the Adam Andrews incident much, or at all, until now. These are the kinds of thing you want to forget. He represents not the best of 9/11 but the worst of it. This was, for me, the first time I saw the grotesque incongruity between the tragic loss and noble heroism from 9/11 and the unconscionable profiteering off it. So fresh from the wounds, and someone was already selling the blood.

You didn't have to do that, Adam. When the plane hit, you didn't run out of the office. You stayed with me to help get every rep out, before you went out. You were heroic. When nobody was looking, Adam Andrews was a hero. When the cameras were on him, Adam Andrews was somebody else. Sadly, his actions were the first of many, made in the name of 9/11, that I found baffling and hurtful.

I want to mention that when John and I first walked out on the set, we got a standing ovation. Then my whole office was introduced, and they got a standing ovation too. To see my reps' faces and how good they felt about everything at a time when I knew they felt awful was very important. Each of them had their own test of survival that day, and they did survive by sticking together. In fact, it was later discovered that we were the office on the highest floor to have everyone survive. That *Oprah Winfrey Show* was as much about them as about anyone that day. I am forever grateful they got that moment.

When the show was over, I waited around to get my package of personal photos back from Roy. He kept me waiting. Maybe he was still salty about my mentioning the kids on air. They said they could mail me the photos, but I said I wanted them now. Apparently, that meant Roy had to go get them, and he wasn't happy about it. After some time, Roy came walking down the stairs and handed me my pictures. I stuck out my hand with a big smile and said, "Thanks, Roy. No hard feelings." We didn't keep in touch.

Back home, everyone was going crazy about Oprah. People who had not actually *seen* the show, *heard* I was on it. Everyone knew about it. (My mother wanted to know why I didn't wear a tie.) Now I knew how big Oprah was. In just two weeks, I had already done a good deal of national media, had been name-dropped by Jim Carrey during the telethon, and recognized by the president of the United States, but *The Oprah Winfrey Show* took it to an entirely new and frenzied level. I also felt that I had an idea of *who* Oprah, the person, was. What she did and how she did it is a model for treating people right in difficult circumstances.

What Oprah did was let us move on as an office. We were *all* recognized. There was something very healing about that. And I didn't realize the power of that type of healing until years later. None of us are alone in this. To be welcomed in Chicago by Chicagoans the way we were—we talked about that a lot when we got back to New York. The sharing helped. On the plane ride back home, I was thinking, *Now we can all get back to life. To normalcy. To business.*

My reps were selling again in October. We hit our quotas. But normalcy? That was a bit much to ask.

Once people hear you were on *Oprah*—well, they don't even know your full story, they just know you were on *Oprah*, and that's good enough. They want a piece of that. And after the incredibly positive experience with Oprah, I decided this *is* worth sharing. I believed it was important to say that in the midst of so much loss—in the wake of so much horror and in honor of so much sacrifice—there is so much value in staying together.

The amount of calls I received was overwhelming. I had no strategy. I just tried to do as much as I could, and do the types of things I thought would do the most good. I had to say no a lot. Some of the offers I said no to didn't make sense to people. I turned down *Larry King, The Today Show, Dateline NBC, Inside Edition*, and many others. It wasn't that I was against major media. In the next twelve months, I would make dozens of media appearances and accept dozens more speaking engagements. The way I decided what to do and what not to do was guided by the following self-imposed standard: Kids and good causes first, everything else second.

It was easy to say yes to the A-T Children's Project. They honored John and me at their annual event in New York City. *A-T* stands for ataxia-telangiectasia, which is a rare, fatal neurodegenerative disease that strikes children. Getting A-T is like getting muscular dystrophy, cystic fibrosis, cerebral palsy, immunodeficiency, and cancer all at the same time. The A-T Children's Project fights this awful disease. Joy and I have been on the New York committee since I was honored in 2002. I plan on being involved with this cause for the rest of my life.

It was easy to say yes to Bethphage, a foundation in Nebraska that helps handicapped adults with everyday living needs in twelve different states. Bethphage is an organization that would provide services for someone like my sister Susan if my sister didn't have us. Joy and I flew out there and met John. David Jacox, the president and CEO of Bethphage, presented us with an award at their annual dinner. There must've been a hundred Bethphage recipients at the event. At one point during the evening, one of the younger recipients took the microphone and sang "God Bless America." If you had been in that room, surrounded by young men and women with varying disabilities and heard that boy sing, you would've truly heard that song for the very first time. When it came time for my remarks, I said to them, "We did something great *one* day, you do something great *every* day." It was a powerful evening.

To top off the weekend, we were the guests of Bethphage at the Oklahoma-Nebraska football game. Coincidentally, my freshman football coach at Brown, Ron Brown, had become an assistant coach at Nebraska. We met on the field after the game. It had been fifteen years since we'd seen each other. We embraced. I saw the emotion in his eyes. This all made sense to me—my connection to him, to all those kids, to my sister, to Tina, to myself.

As soon as I got back home, I shipped six dozen I ♥ NY T-shirts to the Bethphage recipients I met that night.

These were the types of events that brought some logic and sanity to the otherwise-unmanageable state of my psychological and emotional life. It was not just easier to say yes to these invitations, it was one of the only ways I kept it together.

It was easy to say yes to kids. The first "audience" of any kind I spoke to was an auditorium of 150 high school students at Kittatinny Regional High School in Sussex County, New Jersey, in October. Jenn Reynolds, a childhood friend of Jeff Fernandez's wife, taught there. She said the kids were removed from the event. They saw it on TV, but they didn't really feel it. I was hesitant only because I did not know what to say or how to deal with it—what would be appropriate. So I just shared what I remembered. After I spoke, they opened it up for Q&A. That's when I could really see what was on the kids' minds. They all had some personal connection to the day. They knew someone or lost someone, or knew someone who lost someone. One student asked me point-blank, "Were you scared?" They had so many questions, and each question they asked was forward, honest, penetrating. Finally, a student said to me, "What advice can you give to us about thinking about all that happened?" I paused for what was maybe an uncomfortable full minute. I stared at them soberly and spoke in a softer tone, "Look, if I have a message for you, it's this: My office, me, and Tina—we made it out because we decided to look out for each other, right from the start. That's what you have to do. You may not like everybody, but you should look out for each other because you just don't know what's going to happen." They presented me with a big *K* for *Kittatinny* sweatshirt. I walked out of there feeling funny, but Jen thought it was fantastic.

From then on, no speaking engagements were better than schools. With each group of kids, I tried to remember back to when I was a boy and read about big national events and thought, *What if I met someone who was part of that event?* 9/11 had to be frightening and confusing for them. I wanted to offer kids some sense of comfort. I thought the best way to do that was to present a strong front, to let them know that it was going to be OK. Even though in my gut, I felt it wasn't. Maybe in trying to protect them I diverted myself from feeling my own vulnerability. Maybe.

In particular, I'll never forget a trip to the Boys' Latin School of Maryland, in Baltimore. My dad drove down with me. That was a treat. It was the only time when he was part of one of these things. We enjoyed the whole ride down together. The kids took pictures of me and my dad. Again, the biggest thrill was hearing their questions. I could feel their remarkable empathy. These are kids who are so desensitized from TV, video games, commercials. But these kids felt 9/11. I watched my dad sitting in the back of the classroom with a smile on his face, listening to me talk to these boys. I was a Catholic school boy in a uniform myself once. No doubt, my dad was remembering that too.

With each school, I imagined that in the days and weeks and months following 9/11, teachers were bombarded with questions from kids—tough questions. These poor teachers don't have those answers. How do you explain to grade school kids why things like this happen? How do you explain to them why people are jumping out of windows? You know they saw it. You can't prevent them from seeing it. And I imagined teachers tried to counter with, *But did you hear this good story? Instead of the jumpers, how about the guy who carried the woman in the wheelchair? Why don't we sit down and write to him?* I could not say no to that. If I could give that alternative story to what these kids were seeing on TV—fire, planes, blood, funerals, villains, people jumping, running, screaming, crying—if I could take my story to them, then maybe they could walk away with something more than never-ending replayed images of abject terror. And instead of walking away, we could walk forward together. I walked out of every classroom feeling that I had done something useful.

I got a lot of calls to attend annual galas where I would put on a monkey suit, sit, say nothing, stand up, wave, and be acknowledged for what I did. John and I were feted at the Waldorf–Astoria Hotel twice. The first time was at the annual Columbus Citizens Foundation Gala, where Charles Gargano, head of the New York State Economic Development Commission under Governor George Pataki, headed the event. On our second trip to the Waldorf, we were honored guests at the star-studded Christopher & Dana Reeve Foundation for spinal cord injury and paralysis dinner hosted by actress Helen Hunt. They wanted to recognize our helping a disabled, wheelchair-bound person. We stood up, waved, sat down. We shook every hand. Everyone was very nice.

I was deeply touched when Paul Morfogen's father, Zachary Morfogen, asked if I would be his guest at a Brown University dinner given in his honor for his work in the arts. Mr. Morfogen graduated from Brown in 1950, and Paul was my roommate at Brown for two years. Mr. Morfogen was always a man I respected greatly, and it was an enormously fulfilling experience to be paid respect from him like that.

No "appearances" ever matched the feeling I had when the people I knew and loved did things to tell me how much they loved me back. During that busy October, the Sisters of Charity of Saint Elizabeth, who run my old high school, were having their annual dinner at the Madison Hotel in Madison, New Jersey. My grade school principal asked me to be part of that dinner. They were already honoring former New York Yankee greats Yogi Berra, Phil Rizzuto, and Gil McDougald. They apologized for asking at the last minute, but they wanted to put the picture of me and Tina from *People* on the back of their event program. Sister Sheila Holleran was adamant about it. Trust me, you don't beat Sister Sheila in an argument. My whole family attended the event. They publicly acknowledged me. I said a few words, and I saw a lot of people I knew who gave me pats on the back and kisses and hugs. These were my people. These were moments I will never forget.

October was so busy that I couldn't say yes to all the things I really wanted to say yes to.

Angelo had to accept an award given to me by Bergen County (NJ) Department of Disabilities while I was being honored elsewhere across the country.

Every day, my mailbox was full of notes. They came from both sides of the aisle (Ted Kennedy *and* Laura Bush, for example), and from hundreds of complete strangers. I also received a note from my old high school football coach at Immaculate Conception, Lou Racioppe. Lou, who now coaches at Verona High School, handed a note to my mother in the Verona High School cafeteria, and she passed it along to me. In the handwritten note, my old coach told me how proud he was of me. A few months later, when I was inducted into the Immaculate Conception's Sports Hall of Fame, I asked Lou, who is also a member of that Hall of Fame, to introduce me. In his introduction, he spoke about the contents of his note. It would be a mistake to say there wasn't some of Lou Racioppe in me while I was carrying Tina. His words meant a lot to me.

October 2001 was a blur. But I vividly remember carrying my bags off the plane in Boston's Logan Airport, to be honored at the 2001 CompTel awards, the annual expo for the telecom industry.

That Sunday afternoon, just before I flew out, I was with Joy, my parents, my brother and his wife, and my sister and her family, picking pumpkins. Driving back to Jersey City, Joy and I heard on the radio that the United States had declared war on Afghanistan. "Are you really going to fly out tonight?" Joy asked. "Must you?" Things in the world were tense enough as it was. Now this?

I flew into Boston and got to the Sheraton Boston Hotel about 9:30 p.m. I checked in, dragged my bags into the elevator, slid the key in the scanner, plunked my bags down, and turned around to leave the room and meet my Network Plus buddy Rob Norton in the lobby for a nightcap.

Exhausted, I noticed a gift basket on the table with a little card resting against the champagne bottle. I opened it and read the note:

Dear Mr. Benfante:

Since we opened our doors 36 years ago, we've had Presidents, Prime Ministers, Members of Congress, Medal of Honor winners, movie stars and many ordinary folks stay at the Sheraton Boston Hotel. We've never been more proud then we are today to welcome one of the true heroes of the September 11th tragedy.

If I or any member of the team at the Sheraton Boston Hotel can assist you during your brief stay, please let us know.

Doug Ridge
Hotel Manager

I just stared and stared at this little note.

This person went out of his way to write me a personal note. Some guy took his own time. It wasn't in his job description. No boss told him to do it. He just did it. I was so humbled, so shrunk down in size. I said to myself, *I am going to save this note for the rest of my life.* Not because I wanted to show my kids someday: "Hey, look here, I'm compared to prime ministers." Just the opposite. It was one regular guy writing to another regular guy. He wasn't looking for extra points. He didn't even know if he would ever meet me. I bet nobody, except him and me, knew he wrote it. I tried to find him the next day, but he was off. I never got the chance to properly thank him. I do so now. Doug Ridge, you reminded me of what and who matters, and how to act. Your selfless thoughtfulness carried me through the tensions, fear, and confusion of that evening in Boston, just weeks after it had all happened.

Since I had gotten out from under that truck down in the rubble, I had been reacting nonstop every minute—answering every phone call, every interview, flying, driving, talking, bowing, tipping my hat, asking my boss for another day off, Joy asking me not to leave. And then you get a note like that. It just right-sizes you, man. It made me stop and pause. This was no national media network, famous celebrity, or black-tie gala at a five-star hotel. This was a stranger honoring what I "did"— my act—with a simple act of unnecessary, unrequired kindness. That was the best of post-9/11—the thousands of little acts of kindness and relief that echoed the thousands of acts of kindness and relief on 9/11. No fame or wealth is needed to act like that. It's just what you do when no one is asking you to and no one is looking. It just showed how much each of us can matter to each other, the difference we can make. That note that night made all the difference to me.

I had been running from place to place, plane to plane for weeks. So many kindnesses and generosities had been showered upon me. Many excellent words had come out of me, said to many fine people. Yet something inexpressible nagged at me. Something I couldn't locate. There was a hole in me that seemed impossible to fill. Business unfinished.

I knew where I had to go. I just hadn't put down the phone long enough to go there.

A RETURN TO GROUND ZERO

It had been five whole weeks since 9/11. With all that had happened, it seemed paradoxically like forever ago and at the same time something so near to me that I still felt it on my skin.

I had our new office at Network Plus reasonably under control. While I sat in my new office chair in our far West Side location in Chelsea, the collapsed Twin Towers still smoldered blocks away. I found myself bizarrely thinking about random items I'd lost on that old 81st-floor office—a sales trophy I used to give out, photographs I kept in my file cabinet, some books. *Whatever did become of Mike Wright's copy of* Black Hawk Down? I snapped up from my office chair, told everyone I had a client to see, and walked myself down to Ground Zero.

You could only get so close to it, and then security had to pass you through. I got as far as I could, showed the police officer my old Network Plus ID, and said I was meeting my CEO across West Street at the pier behind the World Financial Center. He let me in.

I meandered down as far as I could. I got close to it, maybe thirty feet away. I could see all of the destruction. I could smell it. The ash, the cranes, men in masks with buckets. Contorted steel beams shot up from the debris as if a child had carelessly dropped the contents of his erector set all over a play space— some here and then there, not over there, but all the way back there. Tiny pockets of smoldering remains lay everywhere. *How the hell did I come out of here without a scratch?*

The area and scope of destruction was massive. There was nothing left. The devastation was total. And *I* got out of *there.* Any little piece of anything could've hit me. I imagined fifty different ways, times, and places something could've crushed me. I felt weak thinking about it. I felt so tiny and vulnerable. But *I* made it. All of a sudden, my legs started to give way. *Should I be here? Am I being weird? Morbid?* I wanted to be near it, but the nearness made me less and less steady.

I had to see it. I had to go back. But being there took some- thing big out of me. Because standing in front of it postmortem was a different experience than being there while it happened. Incredibly, it was worse. I viewed it clinically and clear-eyed, and that made it more terrifying. During the day, we were moving. There was no time to assess the entirety of the situation. On the 5th floor, we had an objective: get out. When we got out, we had another objective: get Tina into an ambulance. The moment after I shut the ambulance doors closed and turned around to survey what had happened, there was a camera in my face. The next thing I knew, the building was coming down, and I ran. I didn't get to watch it, focused and informed like the viewers did at home. I saw it all later on TV, of course, but those images didn't connect to my images of that day or those moments.

Standing at Ground Zero five weeks later—surrounded point-blank by the enormity of it and with no objective other than to take it all in—chillingly bridged my singular, subjective journey with the entire, collective 9/11 experience. And it all added up to one simple and overwhelming conclusion: death. What I was looking at was a graveyard, yet, somehow I'd wormed out. More so than any other time, I saw how close to death I had been that day, even more than when I was gagging, terrified under that truck. I didn't like what I was seeing. It gutted me and my sense of self. I felt that I had no armor anymore. The whole world was unsafe, unfair. My identity—I'm strong, I'm fast, I'm smart, I'm a running back—was stripped from me. In an instant my new worldview was fear not strength, mistrust not faith. *The world cannot be counted on.* Everything—my existence—is a crapshoot.

I came to believe that my life to that point had been a myth of control. I thought about everything that happened that morning, starting on the 81st floor. I thought about the thirty or forty things on 9/11 that if I had done instead of not done, or not done instead of done would've left me dead. I thought about all the other lives that started that day, wherever they were, in or around Ground Zero, and how they were not as fortunate as me. I took a few steps back from the makeshift railing girding the construction platform. And I smelled it. It was the same smell of that day, a smell that smelled like nothing else—like many things burning together. Things I did not want to think too much about.

I now understood in my core that the only forces of the universe that held sway were randomness, luck, and indifference. And that it was, above all, beyond my meek powers to control any of it. I could feel myself strangely emptying out on that construction platform. I saw myself not as myself but as a shell, a casing that looked like me but was absent my uniqueness, my purpose.

I caught a couple workers in masks looking up at me. Time to move. I walked the perimeter of the secured area. I passed where Borders used to be. I walked beside Century 21. I wanted to see everything that was there and everything that wasn't. I walked for a good half hour. *Maybe this is the last time I'll come down here.* I picked up my pace, no longer observing but searching. Searching for what, I don't know. I visualized physical things I remembered. Street carts. Newspaper stands. Tables and chairs in the courtyard. The globe fountain. They were all symbols of a time before, when the world still made sense. When I was invincible. When I felt free, not guilty. Clear, not conflicted. Forward-moving, not imbalanced. Mighty, not frail. Meant to be, not accidentally and unjustly, here. I saw none of those symbols down at Ground Zero that day.

I stopped walking and hung myself over the railing, catching my breath. This was surrender. This was where I belonged. I was suddenly hit by the urge to walk down into the pit and dig, shoulder to shoulder, with the men in masks. I could help.

I didn't want to go back to an office or anything separate from this. *This is me. I should do anything I can to give comfort. Maybe it can comfort me?* I shrunk into powerlessness again. *What purpose could I possibly serve here? What purpose am I serving in telecom?* Let's face it, I was selling telephone systems and T1 lines and Internet service. *What am I doing? What am I supposed to do?* I returned to the office that day but told no one where I'd been. Looking around the office, and having been where I'd just been, it was hard to be there. It was getting hard to be anywhere.

These are the feelings I kept from Joy and from my family. Sometimes I would say to Joy, "It's hard to think I got out of there without a scratch." And she would look at me straight-faced as if I was the last one to figure it out. "Yes, Michael. No kidding," she'd say, thinking to herself, *I realize it. You don't. Buddy, you don't even know the trouble you're in.* But I didn't want to hear that from her or anybody. I killed any conversations going there. And most of the conversations going there were started by people who cared about me. I was walling them off, just when I needed them most. Joy wanted me to tell her more. She begged me. But that was all I could share. How it must have hurt her, day after day, conversation after conversation like that. She just wanted me to do whatever it was I had to do to get me back to who I used to be. She thought talking about it would help get me there. She wanted me to see someone. That was the biggest issue. But I never did. That Friday, 9/14, when our office met in New Jersey, they strongly recommended it. They had therapists right there. It was easy to get started. A lot of guys were doing it. Joy knew it would be good for me. I needed to release the guilt and pain I was feeling somehow. Marc Reinstein was seeing a therapist. I'll never forget what he said to me: "Mike, not for nothing, but the reason I want to go now is because I don't want to have to go later." He said he didn't feel like it, or really even so much as want to do it. I kind of laughed it off. "Good for you, bro," I said. *What's he mean "go later"? Later I'll be feeling better.* Time heals all wounds, I was taught. *I just need to get through the now, and I'll be OK.*

But Mark was right. I should've listened.

I thought I was working it out my own way. I was speaking to kids, telling my good story to people. I was also being pulled in a lot of different directions. I know now that all that pulling prevented me from looking inward and thinking about how I felt, how I was affected by the experience. Maybe if I hadn't had all the media attention, I would've done things differently. Maybe. As it was, I lived a strange dichotomy—talking about it publicly but coming home, shutting down, and being tormented by it. When I spoke, I spoke about saving someone else, never about my own fight for survival. The story I was telling people had nothing to do with my terror. I remember speaking to an audience of eight hundred people in an arena in Moline, Illinois, before a Quad City Mallards semi-pro hockey game. I got to the point in my story where I'd say, "Then I saw things you never want to see in your lifetime." That's how I would describe it. Later, in the Q&A, a man asked, "When you said 'things you never want to see in your lifetime,' are you talking about seeing the people jump?" I said yes, but I didn't go into it. I never expanded farther than that. I felt that I shouldn't. I felt that it was disrespectful to those who perished. Nothing stays with me like the memory of those people, the people who jumped. There are a lot of things about that day that make me angry, that I can't get over. To think about the innocent people who were brought to the point of thinking, *Instead of sitting here burning to death, I must jump.* Oh my god. What was going through these people's minds? The thought makes me angry enough to kill. But that's not what I talked about in my speeches. I never talked about *that* with anybody, ever. Think about those people, what it takes to bring somebody to that point. Man, that is evil. I don't mean this in a political way. I am just saying, if the word has any meaning at all, a situation like that is evil. These people just wanted to go to work and have a normal day, and next thing they knew, they're hanging out a window saying a prayer, screaming out a loved one's name or whatever, and jumping. I just wanted to go to work too. I didn't ask for that day. I didn't sign up for it. But I was not brought to the point of jumping out a window. I was there, in the burning building, and I got out.

What now? What was I supposed to do with my survival?

The phone kept ringing.

"WHY DID YOU DO IT?"

I went to every interview, every public appearance carrying all this anger and guilt around with me, even though I couldn't identify those feelings as such or connect them to my experience at the time. Invariably, on every one of these appearances, they asked me the same basic question: "Why did you do it?" When they asked me on the CBS newsmagazine show *48 Hours*, I could no longer hide my *unease* with the question.

The *48 Hours* interviewer, Richard Schlesinger, was a great guy. He really was. But in the middle of a very long interview, he asked me what everyone had already asked. If you watch the video, you can see me shaking my head, like, *I can't believe you're even asking me this*. My response in previous interviews had been, "That's how I was raised," or some variation on that. But I looked at Schlesinger as he asked me the question I had been asked and had answered so many times, and I said, shaking my head, "Look, I acted in the only way I knew how. I don't know what else to say about it. I don't think I'd be able to live with myself if I didn't help her."

Why was this not obvious? "Do you need help?" I asked her. She said, "Yes." So I helped her. I guess I didn't have to ask if she needed help. I could've been like, "Oh, you guys are hanging out here. That's cool. I'm sure someone will be up to help you soon. Bye." Nobody would've said I did anything wrong, I guess. Firemen handle these sorts of things. But something about the situation spoke to me, said, *There is imminent danger. She looks worried, and can I help?* So I just did it.

Sure, I had a choice.

Why'd I make the choice I made? I didn't know any other way to be. What's the big mystery? It's what you're supposed to do, isn't it? After 9/11, I participated in this BBC documentary on human instinct. Why did I have the instinct to help instead of ignore? Was it because my father was that way? Because I was raised that way? Some say the logical thing to do is run from trouble. It's a safety thing. Self-preservation. But I didn't see trouble or inconvenience. My mind worked like this: *How long have you guys been here? It's sixty-eight floors. You need to get out of here. Let's get going.* I didn't do a cost-benefit analysis of my needs versus her needs. I saw myself in a situation *together with her.* We were in the same situation. I left it up to her. If she had said no, who knows what I would have done? But she said yes.

I should've asked my interviewers, "Why are you really asking me that? Is it because you believe that most people would not do what I did?" Maybe I felt that the question itself was cynical and counter to what I believe most people would do and what I saw many do on that day. At the moment of the *48 Hours* interview, I was finding it hard enough living in a world where I survived something so many had not. But I knew then, and I know now,

I would not have been able to live with myself at all if I passed her off and she didn't make it.

Doing *48 Hours* was very different than the other media interviews in another respect. It was a taped show. The interview portion was fine with me, but then the producer, Joe Halderman (nice-enough guy then, he later claimed infamy by blackmailing David Letterman) started asking me to give him some B-roll. "We just want to shoot you walking along the river over here," he'd say, or "Let's film you like you're looking for new office space." It was staged. I felt that this wasn't something I should be doing. I understand what it takes to make a show, but that was hard for me. For me, it wasn't about making a show. For me it was about the message. That day and that moment, I started to feel a distance between what I was doing and the message. And that got me feeling queasy. 9/11 had taken place less than two months earlier. I asked them, "Do I really have to do this—the B-roll?"

The subject matter, 9/11, wasn't entertainment. I didn't want to be a celebrity. I just wanted to be useful. And so many people said my story was helping others. So every media call to me was akin to somebody saying "Can you help?" and me responding the only way I knew how, by saying "Yes." *Sure, Joe, you can film me walking along the river.*

My hectic media schedule had put an increasingly major strain on my relationship with Joy. The kind of public demand I was getting would be tough at any point in any relationship, but we were nine months away from our wedding date, and I had not been around to talk about that or much else. Joy's frustration reached its limit. To make things right, I surprised her by booking a long weekend for us in the Cayman Islands.

She was excited. A vacation meant we could finally be alone uninterrupted, undivided. Away from the media calls, she could see whether the old Michael was still around. She could see whether I still had the ability to focus on her. She needed answers to these questions, and she was looking forward to getting them.

A day later, I got a call from a producer in Germany asking me if I'd consent to being a featured guest on *Menschen 2001*, Germany's enormously popular annual People of the Year program. I called Joy to see if she'd like to change our plans. She hung up on me.

Eventually, Joy's brother talked her into the trip to Germany. We couldn't have had a nicer time. We got there on a Thursday, and our hosts, the production company ZDF, really rolled out the red carpet for us. The shoot was live on Sunday night. We were to fly back on Monday. On Monday morning, we were taking it slow, going out to buy gifts for everyone at home. I don't know when it did, but at some point it dawned on me that I had been reading our return flight information wrong. Standing in a toy store on Friedrichstrasse, I realized we had less than an hour to get to the airport. We were late.

Actually, we were too late. We moved as fast as we could but missed our connecting flight. We'd have to stay the night. I was stressing. I had already missed a day of work and had to get back. Our first-class tickets, purchased by ZDF, were no longer available. I'd have to pay $300 extra to get new tickets, plus pay for a hotel. Nobody at the flight desk could do anything about it. Sorry. Joy was stressed too. She went out to grab a cab while I was still trying to haggle with the airline. Eventually, I gave up and went out to the cab, starting to load our bags in the trunk. I say to Joy, "Wait, I just want to make sure I have my boarding passes for both Berlin and Frankfurt." I go back into the airport and get the guy at the desk to reduce the $300 cost to $150. In the middle of our conversation, he jerks his head up as though someone cattle-prodded him in his ass and stares me straight in the face.

"Mr. Benfante?" he says.

"Yes, Benfante. B-E—"

"Wait a moment please," he says. *Christ, they're gonna nail for me the other $150.* An official-looking woman in a different version of the airline's uniform came out with another guy.

"Mr. Benfante," she says. "This gentlemen over here will take care of you. I am so sorry. I did not see the show last night, but I heard it was marvelous." The fee to change both flights was waived. They rebooked us first class and paid for our hotel. "We are honored to have you flying on Lufthansa Airlines. We didn't realize it was you until one of our staff back there who saw the program recognized you."

I am in Germany. Not Chicago, not Boston—Germany. What is happening?

* * *

Back in New York, as we headed into December, the flood of national media recognition reached a peak. A&E's *Biography* with Harry Smith broadcast their Top Ten Biographies of 2001. Bush was number 1, Giuliani number 2, followed by the NYFD/NYPD at 3, me and John at 4, then Osama bin Laden at 5. What an honor. That list generated a ton of additional attention and media requests. I seriously considered shutting off my phone after that.

Later that month, we reached the pinnacle. Marvel Comics put out a 9/11 collector's edition of *Spider-Man* with an all-black cover. Tina told me about it. They didn't use our names, but they drew two guys carrying a woman in a wheelchair down the tower stairwells. I had to go to Bayonne to get a copy. Unbelievable. It was us. We were in *Spider-Man.*

By the time Christmas arrived, my glorious national profile bore little resemblance to my tense private life. I took off from work the week of Christmas through New Year's. Work had almost become an annoying obstacle in the way of the rest of my life. No longer a private company, Network Plus's stock was tanking. Pressure to meet our numbers no longer came from my CEO but from anxious shareholders and ominous investment banks. The company was no longer like a family but more like a chain gang with no hope of ever pleasing its pit boss. Morale was low.

At home, I had become farther and farther removed from our wedding planning. Joy took it all on her shoulders. That was not easy. She was from Michigan. She didn't know her way around New Jersey like I did. But I was 9/11-consumed. I knew about the wedding checklist items—the band, the deposit, the menu—but I had no real feeling for them. The wedding became *her* thing. The extent that I was available was to whatever extent a wedding plan item was 9/11-related. We were pulling at each other, but in opposite directions. I was always trying to get her to understand what I had to deal with. She would plead with me to understand what she had to deal with. Both of us charged that what the other was dealing with was ultimately only about him or her. Arguments. Strain. Anxiety. Distance. Day by day, the gap in our communication widened. Small rifts enlarged into major differences.

My *fiancée*. How she must've looked at me and thought, *Here we are. I'm going to spend the rest of my life with this guy. We're going to be a team. We're going to start a life together. Planning a wedding together is the first step of our new partnership, which will lead to a family, and this guy is not here for any of it.* Something else completely took over our lives. Well, it took over my life, and she became an involuntary passenger. How many times did I tell her "You just don't understand"? But it is impossible to comprehend that which is not communicated. I was giving her nothing to understand. What about what *she* was going through? I should've made our wedding the priority. I didn't. Joy looked at me and saw a wall, the same one she saw when our eyes first met in the lobby of Robert's Upper East Side apartment building on 9/11; still up but stronger, more layered. I insisted there was no "wall." I argued that people needed to hear my positive story, and that if I was asked, I had to tell it. But I went too far. Joy understood what I had to do, but I went too far. She held in her hurt and did not speak it. But it built up inside of her.

By Christmas 2001, we were two people separately holding in their frustration, confusion, and rage. I was unable to share my pain. She was unable to help me heal that which I did not share. We had to plan a wedding and pay for it. We thanked God on Christmas that I made it out of that tower, but our gratitude competed with our silent frustration. And the phone never stopped ringing.

Things Change

Network Plus folded late January 2002. I got the word directly from our CEO. The company was filing for bankruptcy— Chapter 11 and then Chapter 7. I had to let everybody go. It wasn't exactly a Happy New Year.

Our office goes through 9/11, the trauma. We go on *Oprah*. I get them all, one by one, to come back to work to show this will not defeat us. *This will not defeat us. This is what America is about. This is what our company is about. We're back. We're selling.* It's a different office. Bad location. So what? We can make it work. Then just like that, *boom.* Everybody has to leave. Find another job. No notice. Just a phone call. *You tell them, Mike.* I told them. What the hell? What can you say? What do you feel? What sense is there in the world? Two jet planes and two collapsing towers couldn't break this office up, but corporate mismanagement could. We beat the terrorists, but we couldn't beat the accountants.

We were putting on a wedding in seven months. What did the end of Network Plus mean for me? I was asked to stay on to manage the assets of our office while the company was in receivership. I'd get a modest salary. I couldn't afford not to have a salary. At best, this was a Band-Aid on my financial situation.

Starting in February, I sat by myself in an empty office and coordinated the deconstruction of Network Plus, a company that I helped build. I missed my guys. I remembered our Christmas party a few months prior. I got back from Germany and gave out posters of original Berlin Wall graffiti. The reps presented me with gifts and plaques of appreciation for what we did on 9/11. I felt loved by these people. I felt love for them. We rented out SPQR, a restaurant in Little Italy. We had the whole place. What a special night for us to pause and look at each other. We were more than mere co-workers. The next and last time we got together again as a group was the day I let everyone go. I felt so at a loss in that moment. To all those guys: I always felt that I never did thank you enough.

And that was it. I walked into that empty office every day from February to May. There was no selling. There were no more in days or out days. Instead, I inventoried pencils, paper clips, and tissue boxes. I filed reports.

The media requests and public appearances did not let up. I began, however, to see a change in their character. The first sign of this was when I attended a United States Senate Hearing before the Special Committee on Aging about Emergency Preparedness for the Elderly and Disabled.

Senator Larry Craig headed the committee. He wanted to examine what happened on 9/11 and see what we learned from it. (A few years later, Senator Craig's actions in a public accom-

modation would put him on the other side of the hearing table.)
This was no media interview or black-tie dinner.

I walked in to it feeling that I should've written something
down. I was nervous and unprepared. *Would I get in trouble for
something? What trouble? Who needs this?* I was also embarrassed
by Network Plus having folded and felt reluctant to do much in
public.

It was a field hearing, held in a conference room in NYC. The
impressive array of panelists included the U.S. Department of
Health and Human Services Assistant Secretary for Aging, the
Federal Emergency Management Agency's U.S. Fire Admin-
istrator, the Director of New York City's Office of Emergency
Management, the Associate Director for Epidemiological Science,
National Center for Infectious Diseases, Centers for Disease
Control and Prevention, and New York Congressman Benjamin
A. Gilman. Really, what could I add? Who was I to comment?

I listened to all the experts go before me. I was the second-
to-the-last speaker. I was asked to retell what happened once I
met Tina on the 68th floor and how we got out. I told my story.
After grilling some of the other panelists about the preparedness conditions and responses that day, Senator Craig asked me
some short, perfunctory questions about whether or not Tina's
portable wheelchair was used and whether we'd ever had a fire
drill before 9/11. Then we engaged in the following dialogue:

Senator Craig: Well, Michael, your testimony is special.
I am sure many people have praised you, as they should,
for your help and persistence under those most difficult
circumstances. I think all of us, when we hear people like
you and testimonies given, question ourselves whether
we could've performed as well under those circumstances. My congratulations to you.

Mr. Benfante: Thank you, Senator. Just one more thing.

Senator Craig: Please go ahead.

Mr. Benfante: All things considered, I agree with Congressman Gilman that it was a tremendous emergency response. I know there were many lives lost, but I think just in the way that our Fire Department and Police Department and rescue workers responded, there were more lives saved. It just should be acknowledged.

I guess I may have sounded out of line. The senator was quick to assure me: "Certainly, I am not critical, and I don't know many who are." But they were being critical.

During that hearing, I got the creeping feeling that it was designed more to focus on what we did wrong or what we could have done better that day. They were looking to find fault. They were looking to point a finger at one thing or another that was the reason for the scale of loss, rather than to look at all the right things we did. They should have been listing the ways our fire department, port authority, police, and citizens acted in order to save people. How can we replicate *that?* should've been the question, or at least *a* question, asked. The selfless acts, the nameless sacrifices: What can we take away from those actions?

Let's face it. Most people who died in the Towers were above where the planes crashed. I don't know how any other community could've reacted any better or gotten better results.

Maybe I was too close to it. But I saw those firemen—maybe seventy-five to a hundred of them—marching up the stairs, knowing they were walking into potentially unconquerable danger, hoping to save one life and understanding that their selfless bravery could cost them their own. I saw heroic acts minute

by minute, floor by floor, hundreds of such acts. There was so
much *right* done. I saw it.

This was February 2002. 9/11 was only six months earlier,
but our nation had gotten past its Kumbayah moment. Now,
little by little, everybody was grabbing pieces of 9/11 for other
reasons, their own reasons. The "story" of 9/11 was slowly getting
picked apart, co-opted, externalized. People were hijacking 9/11
to support their own agendas. I wanted my story to represent an
awakening in us. I wanted my story to show how amazing, kind,
and self-sacrificing we all could be in the face of unimaginable
horror. And the only reason I was speaking publicly about it was
because I felt that society's collective consciousness had come to
agree that now was the time for all of us to check ourselves and
realize what is truly important: How precious life is and how we
should not take it for granted. How noble we could be to and
for each other.

It was only six months earlier that everybody seemed united in
the spirit of being good to one another. Volunteers were digging
in the ground to find what remained, and other volunteers
were bringing them food. So many were grieving, and so many
were trying to comfort. "WE ARE ALL AMERICANS," France's *Le
Monde* newspaper declared on 9/12. "This is the end of irony,"
pronounced the editor of *Vanity Fair*. There was unity—unity
of grief, unity of aid, unity of recognition of the sacrifices made
in the Towers by the firemen, by the hostages in the hijacked
planes, at the Pentagon, and in the days of loss and gratitude
that followed.

My point, my whole point, was that I was not the only one. I
wanted to point to the untold and uncountable acts of heroism
on 9/11 and in the days following and say, "Look at who we
really are. Look at who we were on 9/11. Look how we acted

when the fire came. This is the best of us, the best in us. Now let us *be* our best selves, the best nation, the best community every day forward."

But sitting in that hearing, I could sense a current of thought moving in a very different direction. That room sowed seeds of blame and division, not credit and unity. Sadly, it wasn't just that room. It was only six months later, and it was as though the world wanted to forget those good feelings. Being our best selves, the best community demanded too much of us. The window started to close. And thus, I saw the world begin to go back to business as usual.

The "awakening" was only in my head. Corporate America apparently had no ethical epiphanies in the wake of 9/11. Just one month after 9/11, the Enron scandal came to light. The pensions and personal savings of so many good people had been wiped out, and lives were destroyed. Tyco, WorldCom, Adelphia Communications, Arthur Anderson, Qwest Communications, and others led a mind-boggling and seemingly endless parade of titanic corporate criminality.

And you want to talk about irony? One of America's favorite TV shows was a "reality" show called *Survivor*. That's right. It was called *Survivor*. But the way you "survived" was not by helping others and everyone making it out together. Just the opposite. You win in *Survivor* by carefully and strategically deceiving others, by lying and tricking until one person, and only one person, is left. Then you "win." There were three separate versions of this hot reality show in the twelve months following 9/11. Each production rated in the top 10 of America's most watched shows, notching over 20 million viewers each time. These were the "survivors" our country had become interested in. The ongoing but still very fresh story of 9/11 survival had exceeded the national attention span. The reality lessons of 9/11 survival was no match for the lessons of reality television's *Survivor*.

Of course, of course, we had to get back to daily living. But how could we go on living the same way? I looked back on some of my media appearances in the previous six months, and I was flooded with doubt and embarrassment, which slowly fermented into anger. Here I'd been, thinking that the nation really had come together and really did understand and really was sharing in grief and in sacrifice and buying this idea that in the face of the worst of human behavior we saw the best of what we could be. This gave me my license to talk about it. It wasn't easy for me to talk, but I thought this was the moment when we'd all grow together. But it wasn't a national soul-growth moment, or even fifteen minutes of fame. It was fifteen minutes of the pretense of growth and togetherness followed by a mindless resumption of the way it used to be. There was no growth. I can't tell you how alone that made me feel.

And I'd look over at Joy, sitting next to me on the couch, and I knew she felt alone too.

Prior to 9/11, the outside world could never come between me and Joy. That's what made us strong. It was us first, and then other things. Our careers, our friends, our families—all that could be managed, but we came first. Now I was putting whatever I could between us. It was all me. I put up an impenetrable wall. I couldn't face my real feelings, which meant I couldn't sit still and talk honestly with her. It was easier to deal with the outside, not the inside. Inside was anger, guilt, a shattered equilibrium. Inside I was feeling vulnerable and unsure of myself. I was feeling wrong about being here—wrong about surviving from a logical standpoint (*how did I make it?*) and a fairness standpoint (*why me?*). The photographs, the stories were everywhere. So much pain and loss. I wanted bin Laden caught. But would his capture make these feelings go away?* I don't know. Of all these feelings, anger was the easiest to express. Anger was my external self. It separated me from Joy.

Six months before our wedding, the distance between us was growing.

Every day she tried to let me know about what was happening with the wedding. I'd add only the shortest possible answers to create the briefest possible discussion: "Great, sweets," I'd say. "Do whatever you need to. Sounds great. Flowers? Sure. Your uncle can't make it? All right." She's talking about a wedding on September 13, and all I can see is the first anniversary of 9/11. *I just need to get through it.* "Get through it" is not exactly a recipe for a romantic start to a life of marital bliss.

I really can't go on like this.

The phone continues to ring, every day. More offers, more appearances, more media. ABC Family wants to do something? It's got *family* in its name. I'll do it.

I was still talking to kids at schools, but the nature of the interviews had almost completely changed. There's a lot less talking about 9/11 and a lot more B-roll. The appearances I was making were also changing in nature. People were focusing on the wrong things. I didn't feel that I was being effective. I just didn't want to go fill a spot at a memorial or say a few words at somebody's banquet. It was getting confusing. Should I be always talking about 9/11 because it was so important never to

---

*The night before I handed in my final edits on this manuscript, Osama bin Laden was killed by American special forces in Pakistan. Just shy of ten years after 9/11, he was "brought to justice." How did it feel for me so many years later? It was a mix of feelings—welcome relief, honest surprise, some anger, but mostly immense pride in our military and government. Bin Laden's death cannot recover even a fraction of the loss. I know now that whatever I have become since 9/11, whatever growth I have achieved had and has nothing to do with him.

forget? *I will never forget.* It was impossible to move on, but I knew that I needed to, somehow. The only way to do it was to stop associating myself with things having to do with 9/11. That way I'd be forced to deal with my career, my wedding, Joy. Maybe it was time to get back to that.

Things Change Again

In May, another telecom company, which I will call Telco Networks, bought the assets of Network Plus. That meant they bought me too. They offered me a job with them as a regional manager, which meant I'd be managing offices in Buffalo, Syracuse, Albany, and Charlestown, Massachusetts. I was a New York City guy. That's what I knew. Now I had to learn a new territory, new guys in new offices. I had to fly out from my new office in Newark four times a month. The job was different than my old job, but I was different too.

I artlessly navigated new corporate politics—cattiness, gossip, complaining, turf wars. Maybe pre-9/11 this would have been amusing to me. Maybe pre-9/11 I would have played this game and played it well. Now I saw through it—the posturing, the fiefdom crap. *Don't these guys know what's happening in the world right now?* Here I am, watching guys scheming to fuck each other over. Some rep is telling me in a car ride how he told So-and-So in accounting to go screw himself, and all I can remember are people carrying each other through the shambles of hell. I'm still getting calls about 9/11—to talk to groups, media—but these guys at Telco Networks, they don't know about that.

The telecom industry was tanking. But I had a stable income working for Telco Networks. It wasn't as much as I was making with Network Plus, but I could depend on it, and I needed that for the wedding.

The summer flew by, and each day got more intense as we neared our wedding day and the first anniversary of 9/11.

Anniversary. What a word for it.

* * *

Joy and I moved ourselves into a two-bedroom apartment in Jersey City. In September 2002, the phone was ringing even more incessantly than it had in the days just after 9/11.

This is crazy. The pace of my life is crazy. I need to have a normal life. Let me just be with Joy, have a normal job, and start building my life again. That's what I want. Can I let go? Can I let go of 9/11 and just live like I used to live? Can I move past it? Can I just move on?

9/11 One-Year Anniversary

The week of 9/11, Telco Networks sent out a press release media-wide, industry-wide, and company-wide saying how proud they were to have me working for them because of what I did on 9/11. They seemed to really understand how hard it was for me around that time, being asked to do media, and getting married. I told them it was unnecessary to recognize me like that but that it was very nice of them to do it.

September 11, 2002, fell on a Wednesday.

Our wedding guests were arriving. People from twenty-six different states were coming into town. The schedule: Rehearsal dinner on Thursday night, 9/12. Wedding on Friday night, 9/13, and then a party for out-of-town guests on Saturday afternoon, 9/14. We'd be leaving for our honeymoon in Hawaii on Sunday morning, 9/15.

I accepted an interview on CBS's *Early Show* with Dan Rather and Paulette Brown for 9/11. I had interviews lined up all day.

I wanted it to be over. I vowed that after this I'd put it all behind me. I couldn't wait to be on that plane to Hawaii Sunday and start my new life with Joy.

My in-laws-to-be came to Ground Zero with me, outside the set where *The Early Show* was shooting. Also waiting to go on the show was another survivor, a man who had been badly burned. I ignored all the production assistants and producers and spoke with this man for as long as I could. I listened to his story and told him how happy it made me to see him. They took him away to prepare for his appearance. Sadness overwhelmed me when he left. *My god. What the hell am I doing here?*

Soon it was my turn to go on the air. The interview felt forced, awkward. Everything flowed from an obvious production agenda: Question and answer and move it along. It's a year later. Things were colder. Automated. There was less connection to September 11, *2001*. They said the word *anniversary* so many times I imagined some guy in a production meeting pitching an idea: "Morning show—9/11 anniversary. Get that wheelchair-story guy on the show." That's how it felt. Canned. Packaged. I wanted to talk about being thankful just to be there and looking toward moving forward and getting married in a couple of days. I knew they didn't want to talk about that. I tried to mention it, at the end, but it sounded forced. They gave me the hook. I walked off the set feeling as though I had just failed a math quiz.

After that, I had to walk uptown for other interviews. The three-minute anniversary segments one after another left me feeling hollow and fatigued.

I had only one more appearance to do, and it would be like no other I had done that year.

That night, I spoke at a 9/11 memorial service at Our Lady of Mount Carmel Parish in Montclair, New Jersey, our family church—the church where my father was baptized, where I was baptized, and where I'd been an altar boy for seven years. The chapel was packed, standing room only. I looked around and saw everyone I had grown up with. Mothers who had fed me lunch, fathers who had driven me home from football practice, men and women whom I had known since they were girls and boys. I was home. There were no cameras, no production equipment of any kind. I got up to the podium, and I said to everyone, "I'm going to tell this story in its entirety, and it's going to be the last time I do it."

This is it. This is the last time. No more after this.

These were the guys I knew. These were the people I loved. These were the people who had known me since I was a boy. They knew how I was raised. They had a part in it. They knew why the question "Why did you do it?" was a silly question. They were there to hear what I—one of their own—had to say and together memorialize what happened that day. If I had to choose a crowd, person by person, to tell the whole story to, this would be it. And I told all of it. I told what happened to me and how I felt. I told what happened with Tina and what happened after Tina. I told them about running under the truck, the blackness, the helplessness. No one had ever heard that, *that way*, from me before.

I told them everything I could remember and dragged out every emotion I had. I talked for a long time. The church was pin-drop quiet. There were a lot of tears. Tears from me. Tears from others. Before I even got to the podium, I sat in the pew, listening to the congregation sing "Amazing Grace," and I surrendered to the first real cry I'd had in close to a year. My mother was sitting next to me. She knew I was spent. She knew this was the truth of me here in this church, splayed open, emotionally raw. I listened to the words of the hymn. *I was that wretch. I am the wretch. "Through many dangers, toils and snares I have already come . . ."* I was saved.

I sunk my head down between my shoulders so no one could see me crying. I tried to keep it together, tried not to break into pieces. Everything had come to a head that night: a year of so much hurt, confusion, guilt, anger, and distance. It was time to let it all go. All of it. And I unloaded it all up on that pulpit.

My parents had been worried about me the whole year. They knew I had been holding so much in, trying to accommodate media requests, yet sublimating my feelings and keeping things looking good on the outside. This night was about honesty. Finally, and for the first time, I was honest about my experience on 9/11. And I promised myself it would be the last time I'd talk about it. No more speaking after this.

There is no recording of that night. I didn't use notes. I stepped down from the pulpit after speaking for close to an hour. I looked at Joy, I looked at my parents, and then I looked straight ahead. The path was clear to go to my wedding and get on with my life.

The Storybook Ending

The next night, Thursday, September 12, 2002, was our rehearsal dinner at my sister Maria's house in Verona. We were out on the lawn. My mom cooked everything. We hosted people in our wedding party, as well as anybody who had arrived from out of town.

Joy's father is a pastor. Before dinner, we all made a huge circle on the lawn and held hands while he led us in a prayer. We have a beautiful photograph of it. Seeing the important people in our life joined physically and spiritually was a beautiful way to begin our wedding weekend. My father was happy, gliding from guest to guest with his arm around someone everywhere he went. I saw parents talking to parents, friends talking to friends. My heart was happy and slowing down.

I stayed out late that night with Jeff Fernandez, my best man, who dropped me off back at my place in Jersey City. Joy was already fast asleep at her apartment. There were so many things I wanted to say to her right at that moment. Tomorrow, we'd say everything.

Joy and I drove separately to the Pleasantdale Chateau early the next day. She got ready in a separate parlor with her bridesmaids, me with my groomsmen. All arrangements had been made. There was a place for everything, and everything was in its place. Before we knew it, it was time for the ceremony.

Three officiants worked our ceremony: Pastor Reyes Osuna, Monsignor Capozelli, and Father Thomas Petrillo from Our Lady of Mount Carmel. Joy's father incorporated an old Mexican wedding tradition called "lasso," which involves the bride and the groom kneeling down while encompassed in what looks like a huge rosary-bead lasso. As I knelt down in my tux, tied together with Joy by the lasso, I felt for the first time in a long time like a little kid—like a little innocent boy, stripped of all worldly concerns. I actually felt that I was in a circle of protection. I wanted that lasso to envelop us and make us invisible. Kneeling there on that platform, I felt that I was being transported back to my simplest and most fearless form. It peeled away all my hard bark.

I stared at Joy. *This is it. We can start over.* Joy's father gently removed the lasso. We stood and faced each other, our friends seated on the lawn in front of us.

We said "I do." And finally, after all we had been through, we were married.

Joy and I were whisked into a private room, and the cocktail hour began. They sent in things for us to taste. The food was off the charts. Joy's cousin's little daughter, six-year-old Alessandra, wandered in. Joy said, "Let's be alone." I said, "Let her stay."

The three-piece orchestra and vocalist we'd hired for our ceremony continued playing into the cocktail hour. We left our little room and walked out into the grandeur that is the Pleasantdale—a perfectly kept hundred-plus-year-old French château. We pushed open the ballroom doors, which led out to the sprawling lawn set against a perfect, beautiful starlit night. It was like a cinematic peeling away of the curtains: everyone dressed up, drinks, music, laughter. I knew that this was what I wanted, not just what I wanted for my wedding. *This was life.*

Everyone was there. My whole family. Joy's family. All my college buddies—Billy Hayes, Jeff Fernandez, Ruby, Sleepy, Paul Morfogen, Sully, JP, Joe Osborne. Boozer was there. The guys from home—the Lever brothers, the Michura brothers, the McKeowns. The Network Plus gang—Kevin Nichols, Mark Reinstein, Neil Lucente, Felix Kiliski, Ryan Raynor, Heidi Inzerrillo, Scott Jenkins, Rob Norton, John Cerqueira. So many more.

Tina was there with her fiancé, Calvin. She didn't want me to feel obligated to invite her. Same old Tina. We had done so much together during that year. She got to know Joy and got to know me. She followed along with my life, the wedding plans, etc. For that whole year she tried very hard to remain a private person. She didn't like doing interviews. She never wanted to make that big of a deal out of it. But just like on the stairwells of the North Tower, she and I had come too far together. This was no obligation. She was part of my life. And she was part of this perfect day.

I whooped it up. The boys from home, guys from Brown, the gang from Network Plus—I danced with them all. It was everything I ever wanted out of a wedding. The night flew by in a dizzying whirl of dreamy reverie.

The band left, the bar closed, but I couldn't let it end. We took a cooler onto the veranda, still partying with the remaining core. Joy had a migraine headache throughout the entire wedding. I didn't know. She went up to our room, and all the wives were like, *Get up there, buddy.* So I did.

The next day we went to Paul Morfogen's house, where he hosted a barbecue for all of the out-of-town guests.

The following morning we flew out to Hawaii. I got on the plane and said, *That's it. It's all behind me now. This thing that happened, the media, the sleeplessness, the anger, the guilt, the "hero" stuff—it's done. It's time for a new chapter.*

We spent a week in Maui and then a week in Kauai. We hiked the Napali Coast, traveled the Road to Hana, watched the sunset atop Mount Haleakala.

I am refreshed. I am renewed. I am ready to go forward.

Hero gets the girl. Hero gets his life back. Fade to credits.

PART V

WHEN NOBODY'S LOOKING

2003–2006

ACCESS DENIED.

That's all my computer would say to me. I tried to log on. Punched in my password again. Still: ACCESS DENIED.

This was Monday morning, first day back from my honeymoon. I strolled into my office at Telco Networks in Newark, whistling a happy tune. I said good morning to the receptionist, said cheery hellos to everyone in the office, planted myself at my desk. I had gotten in early to get a jump on whatever piled up while I was away. It looked like my first call would be to an IT guy.

The IT guy said I should call the regional manager. I spoke to several regional managers—none of whom made any sense—until one finally said I ought to call our VP. My VP was totally nonchalant. It must've slipped his mind, he said. Then he said the person who was supposed to be in my office when I arrived today should've been there. "Look," he sighed, "I've got to run to a meeting, but here's the bottom line: In the last two weeks"— the two weeks I was on my *honeymoon*—"your sales region was dismantled, which basically means we had to eliminate your position." *Jeezus Christ, I've been fired. I was actually fired before I even walked in the door.* "Sorry, Mike, but I really gotta run."

I was now a married man. Joy and I had moved in together. This was the first day of our new life. No more 9/11 distractions. I was committed to a fresh start and a new career with this company. They'd be my new family, like Network Plus had been.

These fucks. Nobody had even hinted at this. I was with them for the first anniversary of 9/11, just two weeks earlier. Were they planning to fire me then? They wrote a press release using my name: "Look who's working for us! A hero." I thought, *Wow, thanks. Nice, guys.* I sat with them, gave them a bunch of information for the release. "Is it OK with you if we send around this release about you, Mike?" *Sure.* Sounded like a really nice public gesture of accepting me into their fold. It made me even more confident, eager to come back and begin anew.

So sneaky. So thoughtless. I have to tell this news to my new bride, on our first day back from our honeymoon? They *forgot* to tell me? So 9:00 a.m., Monday fucking morning, that's when I find out? Unbelievable. They could've told me, "It's not working." All they had to do was talk to me like a human being.

I stuffed my shit in a box and walked out. That was it.

This was day one of my new life. *This* was day one of putting everything behind me and starting again.

I waited for Joy to get home. She was shocked. I assured her it would be OK. I could work for my buddy Mac doing construction. We'd be fine with money. The situation would be temporary.

Anyway, I was fed up with the white-collar, roller-coaster, go-behind-your-back bullshit. *You can keep that world.* All you had to do was read the newspapers to see that the cascade of corporate scandals was not subsiding—Freddie Mac, Health-South. Every day it was something else, and thousands of poor people lost their shirts. I was having a hard time getting excited about participating in *that world.*

I still went on interviews for telecom sales jobs, but it was tough for me. Hell, I used to be the one conducting the interviews. Yet I'd throw on my suit, pack a folder full of résumés, and endure the transparent, phony, superficial textbook questions. "Michael, where do you see yourself in five years?" *With my wingtips pressing down on your throat.* "Would you say that you're good under pressure?" *Gee, I don't fucking know. Can I tell you a little story about a day called 9/11?*

Did they know my story? I don't know. I had National Public Speaker under the Specials Skills section of my résumé. That piqued no interest. Under Media/Public Appearances I listed *The Oprah Winfrey Show, 48 Hours*, U.S. Senate Special Committee," etc. Not once did one person ask me about it. And I felt it was wrong for me to bring it up, to promote myself as some kind of . . . I don't even know what.

The job interviews didn't pan out. But I know now, looking back, I probably wasn't making the best self-presentation.

I was angry. Everything I saw happening in the world made me crazy. Politics became more and more divisive. Everybody was taking hard lines. Civility was gone, replaced by blame and demonization. Unity had vanished, replaced by ubiquitous protests. Corporate scandals were being revealed left and right. News reports claimed that soldiers were dying because they weren't supplied with sufficient armor. And why did everyone and anyone seem to have their own reality show?

I watched all of this on TV. I read about it in the newspapers. The shock and confusion that had been my mental state in the year following 9/11 had turned, in the subsequent two years, into impatience, rage, and cynicism. The state of the world became increasingly absurd to me. Nothing was making sense. I lost my temper all the time. I was short with Joy, with family members. I became more and more guarded about my 9/11 experience, which was now totally off-limits.

The phone had pretty much stopped ringing. I was done with the whole tour. And this left me without a purpose and desperate for some meaning. I had no idea where to find it.

Shepard Smith at FOX News called me to be on his show. I said OK. Maybe I'd feel better about things if I did it.

I got set up in the studio, we begin the interview, and all of a sudden he shouts, "WAIT! We have breaking news coming in." It startled me. They cut to a report of an oil refinery explosion in Oklahoma. There was fire, a lot of it. They had good video. "Is it terrorism?" Shepard glowered menacingly into the camera. He spent the next forty minutes speculating. I sat there silent in a chair across from him. He never got back to me. That was it. I felt foolish. *Who am I, sitting here with makeup on my face in a television studio? How is this helping people remember the firemen?*

Before and after several commercial breaks, they promoted a special segment airing later that night on Paris Hilton's sex tape scandal. That's what people wanted to hear about.

Two more 9/11's would come and go in 2003 and 2004. Joy and I decided to start our own annual tradition to honor the coinciding anniversaries of 9/11 and our wedding day. We'd go away somewhere, take the day of 9/11 to reflect on 9/11, then celebrate our wedding anniversary. Inevitably, wherever we went on 9/11, we talked about it with people we met, and my story would come out in conversation. We met some truly wonderful people. But I still can't forget, in those two years, overhearing some unsettling comments from people with whom I shared my story. Comments like, "C'mon, who the hell is this guy?" and "You really think *he* was there?" and "That's a big load of bullshit." Yes, it hurt. But what really got to me was that I could see clearly that most people wanted to be done talking about it. Around that time, a phrase had been coined: "9/11 fatigue."

Yeah, that darn 9/11 was pretty inconvenient, wasn't it? We were a couple years removed from it, but that pesky little 9/11 was getting in the way of our having a nice day. It was as if people were complaining, *I was planning a spa vacation over lattes with a friend, and somebody mentioned 9/11. What a bummer.* Well, I'm sorry to bother you, folks, but you can't forget 9/11, and you sure as hell don't piss on it. How often have I heard someone unconsciously clicking the remote control and saying, "Oh, it's just something else on 9/11." Don't say that, and don't say it *like that.* You don't have any idea of the disrespect you're showing people.

I was appalled that for some the visceral reaction to 9/11 was not "Oh my god, how awful," but a cold, analytical "Well, you could've predicted this. That's what you get when nations act a certain way." That's what they *felt.* That was their primary response. No sympathy. No empathy. No feelings of loss. No sense of tragedy. *Thousands of human beings died. Don't you get it?*

"9/11 fatigue." How could it come so soon? Fatigued from what? Did you lose somebody? Were you there? Does watching a segment on Paris Hilton, delighting in the polarizing sound bites of CNN's *Crossfire,* or reading about the plundering of pension funds relieve your fatigue?

The President implored the nation to "Go shopping!" as a meaningful national response to the attack. Is that what 9/11 did—get in the way of our addictive consumerism? Would spending our paychecks at the Gap really be the best way to fight terrorism and honor our dead?

The world was making absolutely no sense to me.

So what did I do? Did I try to resolve anything in my own head? Did I try to progress? No. I decided to get lost.

It's easy to get lost working construction. You're outside. There are no offices, no phones ringing, no e-mail. Just hammers, wood, concrete, jokes, beer, and cash. No shower until after work, maybe, if I wasn't too tired.

I was quick to rationalize my new lifestyle. *I mean, where exactly is the great meaning in the corporate world? People getting so serious with each other over what? Getting a quota met? That's meaning?* This was my fearful and angry mind at work. I could look at any job and say dismissively, "Where is the meaning?" I could make any excuse not to look at the job listings. The truth was I just didn't want to look at myself. I didn't want to go to the center of my trauma and work my way back to balance. I didn't want to find meaning. I didn't want to rebuild my life. It was easier to tear apart everything and everyone else.

This way of thinking gave me no peace. Soon it dawned on me that even after a year of speaking about it publicly and almost three years since it all happened, I still had not really found the meaning in or made any sense of my 9/11 experience. And that tormented me. The defiant but confounding aimlessness of my external life was nothing more than a reflection of my unshared and unresolved internal anguish.

Internalized and unspoken—three years later—I still held on to unhealthy, immobilizing emotions: anger toward the perpetrators, guilt for surviving what others did not, trauma from the fear of imminent death when I was under that truck, and a pervasive feeling that it was all so unfair.

It's three years later. What do I do with this experience? What does it mean?

Some days I would slow it all down. *I'm grateful. I'm alive. I'm not injured. My whole office made it. The woman in the wheelchair made it. It all worked out.* I was supposed to feel thankful, humble, blessed—and I did feel all that—but at same time I was angry. *Yes, I'm alive, but look what it did to me. It brought me to my knees. It made me run for my life. It made me feel as though I was going to die.* Then I'd think about the firemen going up the stairs and that knowing look in their eyes. And I'd imagine every family who lost somebody they loved, and then I'd become angry again—angrier than I was before.

So WHAT are YOU doing about it?

Self-loathing kicked in. It crippled me. I got so fed up with everything going on in the world and in my life and in my crazy head that I was blocked from growing as a human being, from becoming a better person. It hit me like a kidney punch: *Look at me. I'm not making the most of my second chance at life. And I have no idea how to even do it.* Nothing paralyzed me more than that feeling. My survival on 9/11 was all reaction, reaction, reaction. Now, three years later, there was nothing to react to. I just had to live with it, slowly, day by day, hour by hour. How would I move on, move forward?

My wife just wished I would go back to being the person she knew before it all happened. That's who I truly am, *truly was. Because it's not how I was acting.*

And I hated myself for it. I was blowing my second chance. The chance to live that others had died for, that others never got. But I couldn't figure out what to do with it, my second chance. The world I saw, the world I once inhabited so easily seemed foreign and difficult to navigate. And that made me feel that I was doing something wrong, or that there was something wrong with me. The pain of sitting secretly mired in my shame became unbearable.

So I woke up every day and got lost. I got lost working construction. I put myself as far out and away from myself and my feelings as I could. But I went out too far. Way too far.

* * *

This idea of not facing myself as a way to alleviate my pain only made the pain worse. It had nowhere to go. It festered and metastasized and snowballed to the point where no one really wanted to be around me.

It hurt me to hurt others. So I isolated myself. But here's the thing about isolation: It's not just about being alone, by yourself with nobody else there. It's also about feeling alone in a room full of people, people you know, people you love. And there's no lonelier feeling than that. I was in so much pain. I couldn't hide it. My friends, my family, my wife—they all saw it. And they knew one thing for sure: I wasn't going to pull out of this by myself. I needed help. But there was no way anybody was going to tell me this, not unless they wanted an earful of harshness.

Joy saw it in my ever-shortening temper. I was negative all the time. She'd ask me what I thought about something—anything— and she'd get glass-half-empty. *Fuck this* view of things. She saw me look at life with contempt. I'd come home from a job interview—which had become fewer and far between—saying "Screw them anyway" before I knew if I had an offer or not. She kept trying. She'd say, let's go do something fun. I'd think, *Why bother?*

My family tried to give me space. They'd ask Joy, "How's he doing?" All my life they figured I could figure things out and work through them. My mother used to say I always worked best when I was under pressure. But this was a different kind of pressure. This was not a deadline or a game clock running out. This was the pressure of simply being alive and seeing life as a tremendous, negative burden. They wanted to help, but I gave them no openings. My famous line was "I'll figure it out." I made it difficult for them to even bring it up. They always knew me to be a strong-minded person, but a strong-minded person with a confident and get-up-and-go attitude. Now I was strong-minded with anger and cynicism. That's a hard person to talk to.

They urged me to go talk to somebody else, then. *Why?* I felt that I already knew what happened to me. Sure, I was angry about it, but I didn't believe I was in any trouble.

"Michael, have you heard about post-traumatic stress disorder—PTSD?" They'd read it was common among people who had gone through what I had gone through. Joy would tell our friends that I was depressed. My friends would say, "He's not the type." But that's what it was. I was depressed, extremely depressed. I was a portrait of untreated PTSD, though I denied it up and down.

It didn't take a therapist to see how defensive I was. And the best defense is a good offense. So what did I do? I complained about Joy. "She just doesn't understand me, and it's *her* not understanding me that makes me act like this even more," I'd say. "She's always going against me," I insisted.

"Look at me. This isn't full-blown depression."

"Joy's no expert. She's not a clinical psychologist."

"She's only thinking about herself—how it all affects her, not how it all affects me."

"Why was she adding fuel to fire?" I'd say.

"Just have faith in me that I'll correct myself," I'd say to her, "rather than telling me that I'm fucked up, telling me to see somebody. I'm sick of this. How about standing by your fucking man?!"

You say anything and create any argument to avoid examining your own emotional, psychic pain.

One particularly strong argument I would fool myself with was to say that I didn't want to talk about it with Joy and my family because it would upset *them* too much. *They knew what happened. They saw the films. They saw the people jump. They knew it all factually. So why delve into such things? What purpose would it serve to talk about it? Why should I share with them the images of the bodies I saw falling from the sky? So they could have the same nightmares I was having?*

If I did share that with them, I knew it meant I would have to go through it, through my feelings, to tell them. There was no way I was going to go there. Part of me felt that if I did open up and share my true feelings, they'd say, "Wow, he's really messed up. He needs help." This was true, but I didn't want them to worry about me. And if I talked about it with them as often as I was thinking about it, I feared they'd think, "Listen to him. He constantly brings it up. He's not moving on." I wanted them to think I was getting over it.

When I got right down to it, could I accurately explain to them what I really, really felt? Could I describe to them what it really felt like when I heard that building go *pop* behind me and I was like, *Holy shit, I'm fucked. I'm going to die?* Could I really explain how scared I was or the ugliness I saw with my own eyes? I didn't have the tools or the vocabulary to talk about it in terms that could give it its due. I knew—at least I thought I knew—it would eat my parents up to know that I thought I lost them forever and that there was a moment that I feared was my last moment. No, no, no. I didn't want to dig around down there. I didn't want to feel that vulnerability again. *That's what those 9/11 terrorist motherfuckers did to me. They made me feel vulnerable. They took away my invincibility, my ability to see life whole, to see life as good, to simply talk with my parents, my brother, my sisters, my wife. I was forced into these feelings. They put me under that fucking van, scared to lose all of it.*

My friends and my family wanted me to talk about this. So not only did the terrorists put me under that van, but because I survived, they forced me to go back under it and feel those feelings again in order to get past them. I was a thirty-eight-year-old man. I didn't want to feel weak, helpless, scared, lost, or guilty. Talking about it forced me to relive it. Not talking about it forced me to live in fear of having to talk about it.

No, I didn't die. So I had no right to feel that bad, or any bad. But dammit, I did, and it was making everyone else around me feel bad too.

It was often hardest around friends. It sat between us like an elephant in the room. I wanted them to understand what I was going through, and they wanted to understand it too, but how could they understand it if I refused to talk to them about it? Oftentimes, I would be with a friend whom I had not seen in a while, and I'd actually want to talk about it. They knew me. They could see there was something on my mind, but I always felt that whatever the time was that we were together was the wrong time to do it. How was I supposed to broach the subject? Say, "Hey, congratulations on your son's first communion, but let me tell you how fucked up I am"? The frustration and awkwardness was palpable. In these situations, I felt painful distance from friends and from the friendly occasions that brought us together.

That is how alienation feels. You're out with your buddies, and you remember your role in the relationship as the carefree, fun-loving guy, but you can't plug in to it. Something's blocking you. And everyone else is rocking and having a blast, and you say to yourself, *This doesn't seem like so much fun anymore.* I wanted so badly to connect. I would ask Joy, "Why isn't it the same with my friends anymore?" It was because I wasn't the same.

Time and time again I found myself in a room full of friends, feeling totally alone, totally detached. I couldn't relate. Everybody was kicking back, having a drink, talking about the last episode of *Desperate Housewives* or something like that, and I was like, *What?*

March 2004, Sunday afternoon I was at a gathering at a buddy's house when a newsflash scrolled across the bottom of a giant flat screen TV, updating us on the body count from the terrorist bombing in Madrid a few days earlier. Nobody seemed to pay much attention to it, but my buddy standing next to me does. Jangling the ice in his scotch glass, he leans in and small-talks, "That was pretty crazy, huh?" Then he realizes it's me, and we both feel awkward.

*   *   *

I was desperate to change the noise in my head. In May 2004, I gave in. I got a job on Wall Street with a telecom company I will call CityTel. It put me back in New York City, back down-town. I thought maybe it would be like Network Plus.

Much of my relationship with Joy remained unresolved. So much was still left unsaid and unsettled. But we decided that demonstrations of outward normalcy might help us through whatever was failing inside of our marriage. It was all about making life look good on paper. So in October of 2005, we bought a house in Bloomfield, New Jersey, near where I grew up. It was a huge arts and crafts with a Spanish-style roof, on the corner. The place was a handyman's special. We'd really have to do a lot of work on it over time. Thus that house became the symbol of our new commitment to going forward together, an emblem of our new optimism. We can do this, we said.

But you know what's coming, don't you?

CityTel was less than an ideal situation. The guy who hired me hadn't really consulted the CEO on it. I had been sold on the idea that I'd develop an in-house sales team, like I'd done at Network Plus, but CityTel had a culture of dealing with outside sales agents. Immediately, there was tension. I let it go. I was determined to make it work. This was my new beginning.

In short time, people at CityTel caught wind of my 9/11 story. I never mentioned it. Then one afternoon, after I'd been with the company for about a year, the CFO and the COO called me in and asked me to tell them my 9/11 story. I felt extremely reluctant to do so. I'm trying to move past it, I said, quietly. They really wanted to hear it, though. They appeared sincere. I thought that maybe this was a way to connect with them on a human level. But that's not what happened. As I tried earnestly to tell what I remembered, they kept interrupting. It's like they were kids toggling between Reverse and Fast Forward on their DVD player. "W-w-w-w-wait," said the COO. "Tell us again about that body you saw coming out of the sky." Then the CFO just had to know: "Like, did anybody die right in front of you?" It went on like this. They had no interest in the little acts of kindness and selflessness, the anonymous heroic things I saw people do for each other, the things that mattered to me. These guys were just bored and looking for some free entertainment on their coffee break.

It was disgusting. I felt gross.

I came home that night, and I told Joy how bad it was in the office. She rolled her eyes, thinking, *Here we go again.* She was frustrated from night after night of listening to me spew negativity, wishing I'd do something to help myself—talk to someone. "Until you do," she'd say, "nothing is going to satisfy you, Michael." I'd give her the universal "You just don't understand" head shake. Yet it was still me who didn't understand. I refused to say out loud how much I needed to work things out, still fearful to take the painful journey it would require to do so.

Something had to give. Because the journey I took each day to get to work was tearing me open in ways I could no longer ignore. My weekday commute took me right through Ground Zero. I exited the PATH at Chambers Street, walked up the subway steps outside, which puts you on a viewing platform that allowed you to look out over the devastated area. That platform, originally built as a simple area for mourners to pay their quiet respects, had become an all-out, albeit-makeshift, tourist attraction. People from all over the world were making pilgrimages, every day, to Ground Zero.

I could hear them talking, their accents giving away where they might be from. I heard hundreds of conversations. They stood in awe, mostly. Silent. Respectful. They acted as if they were in a cemetery, or a holy place. Some prayed. Others gently placed flowers. I'd see many of them on my ride in, and I watched their reactions carefully as they viewed the entirety of Ground Zero for the first time from the train window. Sometimes I'd be walking behind a group onto the viewing platform and eavesdrop on their conversation. They'd ask questions of each other, tell each other what they knew, what they thought they knew, what they'd read or seen on TV. They hungered to know more. Where was the North Tower? Where was the South Tower? Didn't that use to be where the fountain in the square used to be? *If they only knew.* I just about broke through my skin wanting to interrupt these people and share with them—not share *my* story but tell them simple things: where things were, what it used to be like for me and the friends who were my co-workers. Then I'd get distracted. I thought I heard singing off in the distance. More like chanting maybe. Then I saw it clearly. It was protesting. Protesters became a fixture outside of Ground Zero. There was always something to protest. I didn't want any part of that, from whatever side it came from. I tried instead to focus on the photos of faces—faces of the missing, faces of the dead—thousands of them, fastened to the chain-link fence and posted on construction walls. Notes were taped to some, messages written next to others. Everywhere you looked there were flowers. They sold them, a dollar each, across the street. They sold a lot of things.

Street cart vendors peddled key chains and T-shirts. Knockoff FDNY junk over here, gruesome images over there. People bought this stuff. *Are you going home to put a picture of the two planes crashing into World Trade Center up on your wall? Why would you want to do that?* I tried to ignore it, just walk through it. I could hear people arguing. An old woman pointed her finger at one of the vendors, letting him know she thought it was wrong to do what he was doing. I saw those types of confrontations a lot. Oftentimes I had to hold back from laying into them myself. The disrespect, their callousness was appalling. They were hawking trinkets like they were souvenirs from a horror movie.

Monday through Friday, I took the train back and forth with the tourists. I heard them talking, and I could see what they were taking away from the experience. And my heart sank.

Either they don't get it, or they've forgotten it.

The last time I was down at Ground Zero, before CityTel, was five weeks after the attacks. We were a united community then, a united country. We collectively felt terrible, collectively sought to heal each other, and stood collectively ready to serve.

Just three and a half years later, I stood in a carnival. *Come see where the bodies burned! Where the jumpers jumped! Where the planes hit! The villains! The heroes!* And while all of this was going on, they were arguing about what to build, where to build, if to build, who should build. And nothing was built. The entire two years I commuted through there, I never saw a crane move, a dump truck unloaded, or any work at all.

The site of the 9/11 terrorist attack had not yielded a single physical manifestation of united response. Instead, this "new" Ground Zero had become a crucible for a thousand different and discordant motivations and a thousand divergent and competing agendas. Some people were trying to love and heal, some were trying to learn and get it right, some were trying to call others to account, and some were clearly just trying to make a buck. In many ways, the five blocks of activity at Ground Zero represented, in microcosm, our national political discourse. The media was full of it. Divisiveness and bloody opportunism dominated. Just three and half years later, those seeking reelection were using 9/11 for whatever reason was most politically expedient. Some dropped it as an applause line, others as a throwaway line. Each claimed to know what 9/11 meant to America. This was not a mighty nation rebuilding itself but a 21st-century revival of the Tower of Babel.

Some mornings, I just sat myself down on a bench, debilitated. I was no political scientist, but when I saw what I saw, I couldn't help but think, *It's working. What the terrorists wanted to do is working. We are not rising above it.*

What had we taken from 9/11? Did we become any less greedy, any less self-seeking, any less fame-obsessed?

They hate *our freedom?* Well, what freedom were we exercising exactly? The freedom to siphon each other's paychecks? The freedom to share our most embarrassing secrets on television talk shows? The freedom to obsess over Anna Nicole Smith?

And how are you using your freedom, Michael?

I had unwittingly become part of the carnival. I was a good story. Some people knew me as "the wheelchair guy." In some telecom circles, they knew me as "the guy whose whole office made it out." Some knew me as "the guy who ran from the collapsing building." They saw the video. Some knew me from being on *Oprah*, but didn't remember why.

I'd lost control of it. I always ran into people who wanted to hear my story. Every day I was out in the world, and I couldn't help but meet people. I told my story in bits and pieces, but it never felt right. I didn't see them walking away with the right message. I didn't hear myself delivering the right message.

The *right message* was not only about what I did but about what tens of thousands of others did. It was the message of how we came together for each other in the middle of hell. And it was all being forgotten. No one would remember if this circus continued. Of course, by this point, I got it. There was 9/11 fatigue. How could there not be? It was understandable fatigue from all the wrong images and all the wrong messages being disseminated. It was fatigue from the constant, blaring magnification of division, destruction, inaction. What they showed over and over again, what they dwelled on was every-thing that is negative. But that was only half the story. On 9/11 there were thousands upon thousands of simple, unrecorded, unwittnessed yet unconquerable acts of strength, courage, and kindness. *Please remember. Please remember.* Maybe it was only a few days, or a few weeks, or a couple months. But there was a brief aftermath—a time after it all happened—where we froze and tried to see each other as people, not objects. We cared. And we comforted. We need to take from *that* and go forward. There are survivors. We *all* lived it, and we all survived it—all of us inside and outside the Towers that day, no matter how far outside you were. We cannot focus only on the worst of it, or that's all we'll ever think of it. That's what everyone was taking from it now, what they were selling down there at Ground Zero and in the elections. That's what they were shouting on TV. Epic confusion. Epic conflict. Nobody was talking about how good we were that day, and the next day, and the day after that. I don't know when it happened, but it did happen. At some point, the seeping rot of conflict, selfishness, and self-seeking took over and wiped out what President Bush recognized as our "national character in eloquent acts of sacrifice," and the scores of true heroes mentioned by name during the national 9/11 telethon, and the hugs from Chicagoans in a bar on Rush Street given to every survivor from my New York office, and the crayon-colored cards sent from Mrs. Toussaint's fifth-grade class, and the ultimate, terminal, superheroic-yet-intensely-human sacrifice made by those firemen. *I've got to tell the whole story. I've got to set the record straight. I want to put down every fact I remember before this thing goes any farther. I can't watch one more tourist walk away from Ground Zero and not get this message.*

When I came home that night, Joy was chopping some vegetables on the kitchen counter. I put my hands softly on her shoulders. She turned around, and I said, "I know I don't talk about it with you, and I know you think I need to get some professional help, but I think I want to write this out. I want to write a book and tell everything."

Joy feared this new "project" would just take me to another level of obsession with 9/11. She wanted me to get away from it. She saw us as finally moving on—our new house, my new job. It had been two years of relative stability for us, even though "the old Michael" was still missing. She stared down at the kitchen floor, then raised her eyes to meet mine, looking at me semi-parentally with a mix of love and resignation, forcing a smile. "I'm all for it, honey," she said. "Whatever works." This was January 2006. It was five years later, but maybe I'd finally found a way to give meaning to my surviving 9/11.

PART VI

DEPTH

2006–2008

Reviewing *Lit*, the third book in Mary Karr's autobiograph-
ical trilogy, *The New York Times* columnist Michiko Kakutani
commented critically on the "memoir craze of the late '90s,"
lamenting that "lesser efforts were propelled by the belief that
confession is therapeutic and therapy is redemptive and redemption somehow equals art."

Let me state clearly right now: What follows here is neither
intended to be art, nor will it be a confession. There are things
that happened between me and my wife that I will not share.
There are places I went and things I did that just aren't worth
mentioning. Telling you about it—about every dirty little
secret—will help no one. It will only hurt. I've hurt enough
people already. I've hurt myself. And, *I* did these things. Nobody
else did. I did. I take responsibility. What I want you to know,
what I want you to take my word on, is that things got dark.
That I can tell you.

February 4, 2006

I was feeling pretty good. The CityTel job wasn't perfect, but
it was steady. We were working bit by bit on the new house we'd
bought four months prior. With this new idea to write a book,
I believed I'd found a way to constructively channel my 9/11
experience-slash-trauma.

I looked around the house at some unopened boxes that contained all kinds of stuff from 9/11—video tapes, newspaper clippings, the ash-covered clothes Boozer had rescued from the trash. I wasn't scared of those boxes now.

This will be a good year.

On Saturday, February 4, we threw my parents a fiftieth anniversary party. It was a plan we'd had in the works for some time. We rented a hall, hired a band, invited everybody they ever knew. It was like a second wedding for them. I have to say, it was about as proud and as happy of a moment as we've had as a family. My parents were beaming. Angelo pulled up next me, put his hand on my back, and said, "I've been thinking, Mike. This book—it's going to help you work through things. I really believe it will."

This will be a good year.

On Monday morning, February 6, CityTel let me go. I was fired. Just when I thought I was back in gear, riding high, my life returning to a semblance of normalcy, the rug was pulled out from under me. I figured I had money for the house, for my parents' anniversary party, for moving forward. How could I go home and tell Joy?

Here we go again, she thought. Joy was only human. When I met her, everything was in order. I had a great job. Continuing professional advancement and increasingly greater financial security seemed assured. As soon as we got engaged, 9/11 happened, and everything started going in the opposite direction. Suddenly I had no security, my future was uncertain, and I was financially unstable.

It was as if as soon as I'd asked her to marry me, it all went downhill. I started thinking about that. *What happened?* I started to doubt. I began doubting my relationship. I know Joy did too.

I wasn't just questioning my relationship. I was now questioning everything. I mean *everything*—big, fundamental things.

I questioned the way the world works, the way people treat each other, the way corporate America works, the person I chose to live with, the decision I made to work for Network Plus, which put me in the World Trade Center in the first place. Every move I ever made was under review. *Why? Why? Why?*

My facile conclusion? *Fuck everybody. I don't deserve this shit.*

I kept my firing from CityTel a secret. I didn't tell my family. I relied on the old *Why make them worry?* rationale, a simple disguise for not wanting to face the pain of my own shame, the shame that was built on the deeper, unexamined pain—guilt, fear, trauma—of 9/11. But you can't hide that much pain. Isolation only makes it worse.

I projected anger more fiercely than ever. The few friends I thought might be able to help with a job saw I wasn't myself. At job interviews they sensed my disgust and my isolationist worldview. *I didn't want that job with those idiots, anyway.*

It was all getting to me. I couldn't talk to another jerk in a tie behind a desk asking stupid questions. I couldn't be a "manager," then a "sales manager," then a "regional manager." These things meant nothing to me (as if the only thing that had meaning was what I experienced on 9/11, the meaning of which I had still yet to comprehend). I went back to that old way of thinking and back to construction, where I could get lost, where I was not required to think too much about the past, the future, or even the present. Instead it was work and Miller time, and some days nothing at all. *So what?* I had an excuse. I was still looking for meaning.

The Abyss

Three months passed. I woke up to yet another meaningless morning, a morning in late April. Joy was already at work. I got a call from Angelo. My dad was being rushed to the hospital.

"It doesn't look good, Mike," Angelo said. "It doesn't look good."

I threw on some clothes and rushed to the hospital. I got there before the ambulance did, so I waited outside the ER doors. I saw them take my dad out of the ambulance. My pop. He was unconscious. They wheeled him in. *Not now. Not now. Not now. I still haven't done . . . haven't become . . . haven't said . . .* Angelo is there. He tells me again, "It doesn't look good."

It's happening too fast. He was just at my house the day before. Ever since he retired, he would just show up like that. It was a great thing. I had just gotten a Fisher-Price slide for my niece Angelina, and he was coming to pick it up. He came over. He didn't know I was out of work. Maybe he did and pretended he didn't. He looked out at my deck, nodded his head, and said, "This is going to work for you, Mike. This will be OK." It was almost as if he knew what was coming, and he wanted to let me know I'd be OK.

The next morning, my father was gone. Just like that. No last words. No anything. Boom.

I watched them in the hospital working on him for a while, then calling it. My dad was gone. He was right next to me, but gone.

I cannot have this. This is not real. I spent the last five years walling off real feelings—redirecting them, ignoring them. But this was real. I couldn't *not* feel this. Like an avalanche, like a tidal wave, like I don't know what, it overpowered me. The weak, puny wall I'd built to keep feelings out and others in was no match for this. I had never felt such a loss. And I was feeling every bit of it.

I no longer had my dad there to talk to, to take to lunch. I realized it now, but too late, just how much of what I did was connected to making my father happy and how much making him happy meant to me. It gave me meaning; it endowed me with gravity. It made me happy. So much of what I did was to make him proud. And he was proud. I never recognized how much of that made me, me.

My father: He was my rock. He was my ally. I understood him, and he understood me. He was the guy I admired the most. He was the one thing I could always come back to. Thinking of my dad made me know there was one sure thing in the world. He was the one thing on whom I could rely. He was the last thing in my life that made sense. Without him, the whole equation did not compute.

That was it. I was down—down for the count and completely unmoored. Whatever fuck-this-fuck-everybody approach to living I'd been working on, well, it was about to be taken to a frightening new level.

My father's absence heightened every anxiety in me. I had never realized how much I stood on his shoulders. It wasn't about needing him. It was about enjoying his love. It was a love that simplified things. It gave me sense and order. It gave me a base. No more. The chair got kicked out from under me.

The suddenness of his passing made for a chaotic time. I bucked up for the preparations, helped organized the funeral and the wake, helped my mom. I did what had to be done. And then, after there was nothing more to do and nowhere else to be, it was all-out emptiness. Just all-out *I don't give a shit about anything—not one single thing—anymore*. I walked the path of least resistance. Self-medication. I mean alcohol. A lot of it. Other things too. Whatever it took. Wherever it took me. Reaching for anything that would kill my feelings. I wanted out of my skin. And I got out. For days sometimes. Sometimes longer. I didn't want to think or feel anything.

Fuck it.

Somebody told me around that time, when you lose a parent for the first time is when you truly become an adult. Really? I felt that when I lost him I was becoming less of me than I'd ever been. I didn't know who I was anymore. I could not see what made me, me. I disbelieved that there ever were any positive pieces of me. *Was I a good person? Did I do a good thing on 9/11? It was all a bunch of bullshit. The whole thing was just coincidence—an accident that put a useless fuck like me in a situation where I did something, not really thinking too much about it, and it made me look like someone I'm not. I'm no hero, I'm a fraud. I was never—even before 9/11—never the son, the athlete, the student I thought I was.* You want to know what self-loathing looks like?

Selfish, self-absorbed, self-loathing.

My wife? My family? I had no conflict with them now, because I had no presence. I simply was not there. I didn't disagree or fight with anyone because I just didn't care. But that just led to more conflicts. My pat answer to everything was "I don't want to be bothered." Nothing *bothers* someone who cares about you more than you saying that. In truth, everything bothered me.

Intellectually, I understood that I was digging myself deeper and deeper into a hole in every aspect of my life: socially, financially, emotionally, physically. But my rationale for living was no longer rational. I wanted to see just how deep of a hole I could bury myself in and still get out, as if simply waking up the next day was "getting out." Somehow I equated self-destruction with industriousness. Anything that required real effort and real responsibility, I just turned my head away. I didn't care about the house anymore. I didn't want to fix it. I was, in short, living a life that was everything my life pre-9/11 was not. All the things that were most important to me, the things I once gave the most energy for—family, friends, career—were the things I wanted to evade and ignore.

And in the middle of this descent into the abyss, Joy tells me she's eight weeks pregnant.

What strength and patience. All this time, while I became more and more difficult, more and more unavailable, Joy kept trying. She believed that we could, and would, overcome. She continued to live life with vision and hope. She continued to be my loving wife.

July 9, 2006, was my birthday. Joy took me to dinner in New York City, at La Kitchenette, on the West Side. Sitting at the table, she says, "I have two surprises for you. Here's your first." She hands me a beautiful birthday card. The waitress comes over, and I order calves brains. (*Calves brains? Why not.*) They bring us our meals. I dig in. "Ready for your next surprise?" she asks. "Sure," I say, chewing my calves brains. She takes out a portable CD player and puts headphones on me. The music plays, and I hear the words "Three is a magic number." It's an old Lou Donaldson tune from a collection of '60s blues music we listened to often. I listened and looked over at Joy. She's got this grin on her face, her eyebrows raised, looking back at me like, *Don't you get it?* And I'm looking at her like, *Get what?* She starts singing along, "Man and woman have little baby, yes, it's three, three in the family . . . three is a magic number." I'm still clueless. The smile on her face just gets bigger and bigger. And I am like, *What in the world are you talking about?* She shakes her head, says, "Listen to the words, Michael." Oh my god. I got it.

We reached across the table, held hands, and for one night let ourselves celebrate life.

I'd like to tell you that in the next seven months I climbed up out of my emotional dumpster and rose to the call of duty. I did not. If I had been waiting for something in my life in which I could take meaningful part, this was it. But instead of being a part of it, I made myself apart from it.

Joy did everything: She read all the books, did the Lamaze classes, and made all the requisite doctor's visits, essentially without me. I was there physically for all of it, but I was not in it with her, let alone make it at all special. I saw these as things I needed to get done and over with, so I could go do what I wanted to do.

And what was that, exactly? It certainly wasn't to go look for a job or pull myself together, prepare for what was about to come. No, I just wanted to self-medicate. I wasn't in mourning anymore. I was an addict—a misery addict. My primary treatment for that addiction was alcohol. Another particularly consistent element of my treatment required my being absent as much as possible—absent even if I was sitting right next to you.

A pregnant wife is not someone you can skate by, give just a little attention. I gave little attention, and I got plenty of feedback on my shortcomings as a husband and caretaker. For seven months, our relationship became a simple pattern of Joy needing and me pretending. That made for seven months of mounting tension.

But this was a process I could not reverse. My absence notwithstanding, Joy's pregnancy progressed, and on March 5, 2007, my son was born at New York-Presbyterian/Weill-Cornell Medical Center. We named him Michael Reyes after both of his grandfathers.

After a few days, Joy and the baby were released to come home. Now there were definitely three in the family.

* * *

Right after 9/11, I had grappled with anger and guilt, derailing my professional career and leaving me questioning whether anything had meaning. After my father passed away, I lost interest in figuring any of that out. *Fuck it* was my answer to problems. *Leave me alone* was my answer to people.

The arrival of little Michael didn't change my mode of operation.

I thought I could keep that frame of mind and still be a father. I thought, *OK, it's just another thing I've got to do. I can be physically there, go to parties, go through the motions. Then I can go out and drown my pain.* It didn't work. I was spiraling faster and deeper emotionally, psychologically, downward financially. Life became harder, and the harder it was, the farther and farther I removed myself.

Emotionally and psychologically, I had checked out long ago. Then, ultimately, I stopped physically showing up for things.

How could that work? I now had a child that relied on me for everything. I had a wife who needed me to be there for her, and if not for her, at least for the child. Our house that was once an emblem of unity and optimism became a huge vestibule of acrimony and burden.

Joy and I didn't sleep for three months. The child needed us day and night. Joy was home on ninety-day maternity leave, and I took that as an opportunity to work more construction, which was really more like doing some half-day jobs with buddies and hanging out, which became working half-days every other day. "Joy's gonna go back to work soon," I'd tell them. "Then what?" Nobody really answered. They'd change the subject. I should've been getting more organized and more directed. Instead, I was becoming more disorganized and misdirected.

Joy went back to work in June. She had to, because we needed the money. I got my mother to watch Michael so I could "work" construction. My mother couldn't really quit her job at the school cafeteria in the fall, though, so I hired a nanny to watch Michael full-time. Soon it became clear the nanny was making more than we could afford to pay.

The spiral deepened—financially, emotionally, psychologically. I was drinking all the time. I was drinking at work, after work. On the days I didn't work, I'd go meet guys I worked with to hang out and drink. I'd come home with booze on my clothes, in my head, and in my talk. My plan for the next day was nothing but the same. That's if I had a plan at all.

But I have a son. I have a son.

Did I use the word *abyss* earlier? Now I'm living below the abyss.

Never had I felt more alienated from everyone and everything. I looked at the world, and more than ever I felt that nobody—not my wife, my family, my friends—nobody gets it. *They wouldn't even if I tried to explain it.* Explain what, though? I wasn't even sure anymore. I needed a drink.

I became a curmudgeon, the downer, the cynic. I was the guy in the room who watched the news and yelled at the TV, the guy who read the newspaper and griped indignantly. I constantly vented disgust. It was all disgust all the time.

Joy had had enough. "How much can we take?" she asked me. "We have a child. You cannot be like this around him."

But I still had my excuse, my get-out-of-jail-free card. I was in 9/11. That meant I was entitled to be overwhelmed. I had special license that allowed me to find everything meaningless. I earned the privilege to sit around every day amid a sea of question marks. If I wanted to avoid, delay, prolong, re-purpose, redirect, or drink away my pain, that was my right. Woe is me.

What utter bullshit.

Nobody was calling about 9/11 or anything else anymore.

Joy sat me down. "Listen to me, Michael," she said. "When I first met you, you were a glass-half-full kind of guy—the most positive person in the room. That's who you always were, wherever you were. You are now totally the opposite of that person, and 9/11 was where it all changed. Just after 9/11, you at least thought you were a lucky person. You thought that 9/11 was a reason for you and others to be even more grateful and more appreciative of all the little things in life. That's not who you are now. You are angry and bitter. You fought so hard to get yourself and Tina out of that building. You fought so hard to stay alive while you were choking under that truck. And you did stay alive. Here we are, years later: There's no smoke, no fire, no building collapsing around you, but you're letting it crush you. You're not even trying to beat it."

She was right. This is not who I was the moment I met Tina. In the moment I encountered Tina, I was a man of action. Now I was a man of inaction. Worse, I was the one who needed to be carried out. If I found myself at that moment in a situation to carry someone out of a burning building, would I have done it? Could I say in an interview now "I knew no other way to be"? The question was too painful to pose to myself.

9/11: How could the one day that exemplified who I was take me as far away as possible from who I was?

This was rock bottom for me. I could go no lower. I had become a person that was so far from the person he used to be that I was not just unrecognizable but I was completely the opposite of the person I was—the person Joy knew and fell in love with before 9/11. How did I get to this place? I got here because the new person I had become was built on all these new feelings—denial, anger, guilt, blame, mistrust, and other defense mechanisms—that were a result of not dealing with the original, unresolved feelings, not dealing with my fear. What does a fearful, traumatized person do with his fear and trauma when it's too great for him to face? He piles bullshit on top of it. That way you can fool yourself into thinking it's not really there. You've paved it over with so much bullshit you can't even remember what those scary feelings were or why you have to work so hard to hide them. And after you've piled enough bullshit up to cover those original unresolved, untreated feelings, it's inevitable what you eventually become. Gradually, overtime, day by day, you become that bullshit. You become something so foreign to who you used to be or once wanted to be. You become what I was at that moment: a person who had lost his code.

"You've gone too far, Michael," Joy said. "Either you figure it out, or we find a different way." I knew what she meant. I could lose everything—Joy, little Michael, all of it. I had to change, but I had no idea how. I was terrified. I felt as if I was under that truck again, gasping for air, terrified that I was going to lose it all. My anger, my bitterness, my guilt, *my bullshit*—that was all I had. That's what scotch-taped me together in this insane world. *And who the hell is she to make ultimatums?*

But my son. My son.

PART VII

WE'RE IN THIS TOGETHER

2008–2011

The next morning, they called me for construction—a half-day job working on a back deck in Montclair. We had no nanny. I'd have to stay with Michael.

The little guy was running around pretty good by this time. It was an early October morning. Not too cool, but the season was changing. The sun was out. I unfolded a lawn chair, nursed a coffee, and watched Michael kick his favorite ball around the backyard.

Michael created a little game for himself in which he'd kick the ball against the side of the garage, making a little *boom* sound, which amused him to no end. He did it again and again, squealing in delight each time he made the *boom*. Every other kick, he looked up to me for approval, or maybe just to see if I was still watching. I was watching. My neighbor next door was watching too. Holding a rake in his gloved hands, he nodded to me, smiling toward little Michael.

I smiled back. Michael smiled back too. We all continued smiling at each other—Michael kicking, my neighbor raking, me sipping coffee.

I squinted up at the sun. Was it getting warmer? I looked at Michael, who giggled. My neighbor raised his eyebrows at me and nodded his head. I couldn't help it. I cracked a big toothy smile. My shoulders relaxed a little. I felt the sun on the side of my face, pleasant and warm. I could really taste my coffee this morning. It was a good first cup. The air outside smelled fresh, that familiar subtle smokiness of leaves first drying in the earliest of autumn. I heard the birds.

I looked again at Michael and then again at my friendly neighbor, who was looking at Michael and then smiling at me, and to himself. And I felt . . . good. Really good. In that instant, a rush of feelings overwhelmed me. All at once everything came into focus—my father, my family, Joy, 9/11. I could see it all perfectly—all I had been through, seen, and done. I saw the answer—the key to unlock me from my torment, free me from my exile, and set me on my road back to myself, my friends, my family, my wife, my life. It was clear. How had I forgotten it? It was the same simple truth I understood the moment I saw a woman sitting still in her wheelchair on the 68th floor:

All we have is each other.

That's how we get through this.

It's the one true thing my father taught me that I can pass on to my son. It's the forgotten truth of 9/11, which forced us to truly see each other through the masks of boss or employee or competitor or cultural adversary or anonymous Internet antagonist. And in truly seeing each other, we saw that all we had, if we were to make it through this—through the fire—was each other. I saw that in the stairwells on 9/11. I saw it in this moment now with my son, in his face. I saw it in the face of my next-door neighbor. *All we have is each other.*

All these years I was asking, why? I flailed, prayed, and begged for answers. There were no answers, except one: I don't need answers. I just need to do the next right thing. I just need to remember what was good in the first place: help people. Stop looking for meaning. Stop looking for the *why*. There is no answer. There is just the doing.

All those years I struggled to find a "message."

All those groups I spoke to, all those survivors I met, the television shows, all the kind words showered on me. I was only *hearing* what the message was but not remembering what the *feeling* was. I'm talking about the feeling I got seeing the many, many acts of kindness that day by people you'll never hear about and people I'll probably never see again. The Hasidic man who wiped my soot-covered face, the Asian man who charged bravely up the stairs to aid a firefighter when everyone else was heading down, the hundreds of firemen who made everyone feel like it was going to be OK, when they knew it wouldn't be and they wouldn't be. The *feeling* I had when I asked Tina if she needed help and she answered "yes." *That feeling* was where the message could be found.

The message of 9/11 that desperately needs remembering is no more complicated than *We're in this together.* The *this* means this office, this classroom, this street, this town, this country, or wherever you find yourself standing. And we need not wait for the next fire, the next explosion, or the next tragedy to find that out or to act that out.

That's what was bothering me. It seemed all anyone took from 9/11 was what we had lost. And in doing that, what we also lost—obscured by the mists of political posturing, spiritual grandstanding, and, understandably, buried beneath ceaseless waves of grief—were my actions and the selfless acts of so many others. What we lost was a window of opportunity for all of us who survived—whether you were a survivor who was in the Towers or watching on CNN in Des Moines—to stop and reassess who we were, where we were going, and who we wanted to be. What traumatized me as much or more than the day itself, was how quickly that window closed.

It was as if 9/11 happened, and then, for only a brief moment—during and shortly after the tragedy—the world stopped being a discordant mass of a billion competing and conflicting agendas and remembered its common humanity. But then the world quickly, unconsciously returned to business as usual.

That killed me. I really believed 9/11 would stand as a titanic wake-up call for everyone, everywhere to become better people. But just seconds after the alarm went off, incredulously, heart-breakingly, I witnessed the world fall back to sleep. The media grew more scandal-obsessed, politics became more divisive, corporate greed reached new levels of egregiousness.

That's the world that was calling me a "hero" for what I did. *That's* the world that was asking me to be on its television programs, talk to its children, and testify at its hearings. And at the same time, that same world continued to move in diametric opposition to the "heroic" thing I did. That's what confused me.

I was there in the Towers, surrounded by the unspeakably real death and destruction, but also witness to incredibly true and present acts of sacrifice and heroism.

On 9/11 I didn't check the political affiliation, classify the social rank, or evaluate the business advantage of the woman I saw marooned in a wheelchair. Neither did the man who sensed my panic under that truck and assured me I'd be OK. Neither did the firemen. I was there. I saw it. I know how much good we have in us. How much we are capable of doing for each other. How quickly, if we really want to, we can remove the masks, shed our team uniforms, forget what side we're on, and *be in it together.*

All this time I hadn't been focusing on the right stories—the stories of people who, like me on 9/11, got up, went to work, expected nothing, and acted the only way they knew how to, which made them heroes. And the way they chose to be heroic made perfect sense to me.

I admired Chesley Sullenberger, who refused an invitation to go on *The Today Show* twenty-four hours after he heroically landed a jet plane on the Hudson River, saving his passengers and crew. The media couldn't understand why he was "unavailable for comment." I did. The man just went through a traumatic, life-threatening experience. His wife would not take questions either. She and their children just learned that Sullenberger had narrowly escaped death—something they must've feared every time he took to the skies. They did not want to bask in glory, in fame. They were in shock. They were questioning the very meaning of life, the value of existence. When Sullenberger finally did take some questions, he said, "I was just doing what I was trained to do. Doing my job." He did not self-consciously seek anything in his heroic moment. He simply acted in the only way he knew how, which was a state of mind and a state of action he inhabited every day prior to that moment.

I read with awe how Liviu Librescu, a seventy-five-year-old engineering professor at Virginia Tech University, heard the gunshots and blocked a door to prevent the gunman from entering his classroom while some students took cover underneath desks and others leaped out of windows. He saved all his students. He died doing it. Liviu Librescu was a Holocaust survivor. If ever there was a person who understood the value of life, and living—a man whom no one could blame if he had chosen not to block bullets with his body—it was Liviu Librescu. But I don't think Liviu Librescu made any such complex determinations when he heard the gunshots. He simply acted in the only way he knew how, based on who he was, where he'd been, and who he had become as a result of those experiences. I wish I'd known him. I wish we'd all known him. His students will never forget him.

I loved the story of Chad Lindsey, an Off-Broadway performer on his way to work, who jumped down onto the subway tracks to rescue a man who had fallen. After hoisting the unconscious victim back up on the platform to safety, Lindsey—covered in blood and dirt from the track—exited the station, went home, and continued on with his day. Nobody knew his name until one of Lindsey's friends felt compelled to disclose it to a *New York Times* blog. Lindsey, of course, did not know the name of the man he saved, but he didn't seem to think it was the most important thing. All the aspiring actor could say was "It was quite a New York day." And that's it. There's nothing else. He was simply being himself. What else was he supposed to do? Who else was he supposed to be? It was nothing to fight about or get famous about.

Not everything is a reality show. Not everything is a brand. Not everything is transactional. Not everything is political.

Looking at my son, and my neighbor—the three of us connecting—it came back to me: *that feeling.*

It was the same feeling I got in the forty-eight hours just after 9/11, when the world stood still. We stopped to take care of each other. We paused to take stock of what was really important. We came to each other's aid without consideration for skin color, political party, sexual orientation, or income level. Ten years later, have we kept the promises we made to ourselves in those first forty-eight hours? Have we learned anything? Did we change?

Do we need the fire to come again to show us what we forgot?

Do we need the fire to come again to show us that the mother who loses her house through a sub-prime mortgage collateralized debt scam could be the same woman who gives *your* mother CPR?

Do we need the fire to come again to remind you that one of the men you are downsizing today may be the man who carries you—or your wife or your daughter—out of a burning building?

Do we need the fire to come again to show you how easily it could be someone you know and love who dies on the bridge when it breaks because we did not fix it when we knew it was broken?

Do we need the fire to come again to remind a cabdriver that the passenger whose fare he's gouging might be the one who takes a bullet to save him from the carjacker?

Do we need the fire to come again to show us that if we do not care for our veterans, it speaks of how we will care for each other when it gets harder to give *that* care?

Do we need the fire to come again to make it crystal clear that when you're helping each other down the tower stairwells or getting sick searching in the ashes for other people's remains, no one will care if you're for or against same-sex marriage?

Do we need the fire to come again to teach elected members of Congress civility—that it helps nothing and no one to shout "LIAR!" at the president of the United States during his State of the Union Address? Do you really believe that the president— whoever he or she may be—would not wipe your child's eyes and you would not do same for his child when the fire comes?

I don't need the fire to come again. I don't need to be reminded.

I thought I did. But I don't.

I thought you did too. But you don't.

I know it's in you. I know you would do the same thing that I did. I saw it done by so many. I only wish I could make you realize it has nothing to do with the fire. I carried Tina Hansen because it's what I knew to do *before* the fire. Like Chesley Sullenberger, like Liviu Librescu, like Chad Lindsey, I just got up one morning—September 11, 2001—went to work and did what I knew to be right. That's who I was when I met Tina Hansen on the 68th floor. That's who I want to be again. *That's who I am.* I just got lost, mixed up, and very scared.

It took me these last ten years to remember and realize that all I need to do is *what I did.* There's no grander meaning, no ultimate message. I wasted so much time. I damaged so much I must now repair. But I will repair it. I will make amends. I will use my time. Because that's the gift of now. I can be that person right now. I can change now. I can act the right way right now, here, sitting in my backyard with my neighbor and my son. We were in this together.

That feeling.

We're OK. We really are. In the face of the worst, we were so good. Imagine how good we can be when we don't have to battle tragedy to get there. I know it now. I don't need anyone to tell me. I know. I was there. I saw it. I saw how good we can be to each other.

The only reason I got called a hero is because I got caught doing what so many others did as well. There were over three thousand lives needlessly taken from us on 9/11. But you must remember that there were also over one hundred thousand acts—99 percent of them anonymous and undocumented—of comfort and aid and bravery and sacrifice and kindness that day. Those people were *all* heroes. Heroes like there were in Oklahoma City, London, Madrid, Virginia Tech, Mumbai, Bali, Fort Hood, Tucson. Heroes the cameras never saw. And I don't think it was the first time any of those heroes did those kinds of heroic acts. I bet they did them every day before that moment and still do them, every day, when nobody's looking.

That's how I want to move forward with 9/11. I want to go back to doing it, to *being* it every day, with no big deal attached. When we think of 9/11, I want us to remember how for forty-eight hours the whole world froze and took account of the high place that goodness, love, and togetherness can have in our lives. And I want us to remember how easy it is to flick on that switch and be that person, to be a hero, right now.

That feeling.

That morning, in my yard, I stopped searching for meaning and started to live it again. Meaning was right where I was standing. Meaning is in everything everywhere. And there, that morning, with my son and my neighbor, I found relief. I found peace.

I leave it to others to debate what 9/11 means. I'm a survivor of 9/11. And if you're reading this, so are you. You might not have been in the Towers with me, or near the Pentagon, but you were somewhere. And there is something going forward that we can do with our survival. We can decide right now, together, to be better to each other.

Others can tell the world what is right, wrong, how they know and don't know and what we should and shouldn't be doing. Not me. That's not my job. It never was. If I'm ever going to be a "hero" again, I know what I need to do. I'm going to visit my sister, help my mother, share with my friends, see if my wife needs anything. I'm going outside to be with my son.

EPILOGUE: TO BE CONTINUED

I'VE BEEN READING and rereading what I've written in this manuscript. I promised in the beginning that I'd try to get it right, to get down all I remembered the way I knew it to be.

As I write these last few pages now, I know the end of this book is not the end of my story. There's just a little more I need to tell you.

First, you should know that I'm still scared. Things I see and hear and read still get to me. I still have nightmares. But like my father used to tell me, and like I'll tell my son, when you wake up from a bad dream and the fear won't let you sleep, try instead to think about the good things you know are true.

Counted among my good things is the story of my father telling the doctors that his first child, born with Down syndrome, would be coming home—his home, not an institution—to live with him. I also have the vision of my Network Plus co-workers helping each other out of that building and making sure everyone made it out, everyone. I have the gift of Brian "Boozer" Wenrich, dusting me off, handing me fresh clothes, and feeding me on my way out of that mess. I have the memory of a disabled boy singing "God Bless America" and the knowledge of what Bethphage does for him and hundreds like him every day of their lives. And I have all those images of the heroes of 9/11.

As much as there is from 9/11 to haunt me and horrify me, I have more—so much more—that ennobles me, teaches me, inspires me, and restores me.

That's how I find my way back to rest. That's how I find my way back to the people I love and break free from feelings of alienation. That's how I let go of the guilt of survival and the anger of victimhood, replacing it with energy—joyful energy—focusing instead on what I am able to give.

It's coming. I know the fire is coming again. That's life. But I know now not to mistake what I do in the fire as some kind of defining moment. It's just another moment, in the endless and constant chain of moments, each as important as the next, where I get to define and redefine and define again who I am.

What proved true on 9/11 is what proves true now. It must be retold. This is my part. I have told you what I know, what I saw, and what I did. And I live today the best way I know how—a way taught to me by a thousand teachers that day ten years ago in the World Trade Center.

Lord knows I'm not perfect. I'm still a work in progress, and I've got a lot I need to do. I can't tell you the "old Michael" is back, but I know *this Michael* is here. He's definitely here. And if I'm going to be anything, I am going to honor—not fear—the memory of that day with my survival.

So I go to work in the mornings to my new job, and I try to be a good employee. I come home at night and try to be a good father and husband. I take care around my family to talk kindly and to give love. I see friends, and I let them know me again.

The end of this book is not the end of my story. Another 9/11 will come and go. Then another. Ten years later. Twenty years later. One hundred years later. My story continues, just like it does for all of us. We're in this together.

OFFICIAL PROPOSAL: 9/11 NATIONAL DAY OF SERVICE

IN THE AFTERMATH of 9/11, a general complaint often heard was that except for the soldiers, nobody asked us—our nation—to sacrifice, to give of ourselves, or give up something. There was no call to national service in response to the tragedy. I would like to make that call now.

9/11 was the worst attack ever on American soil. To this day, there is no formal, official national observance. There is no united national symbolic gesture. For example, on Memorial Day we hang flags. On Independence Day we set off fireworks. Here is what I propose we do for 9/11:

As I have stressed in this book, 9/11 showed as much as anything that there are enormous untapped reservoirs of extraordinary human kindness and giving just waiting for a trigger. Though three thousand people tragically lost their lives on 9/11, many more thousands who were not caught on camera and whose names we shall never know showed countless acts of courage, dignity, comfort, and selflessness. On that day, an act that manifested from the worst of humanity's capabilities activated the best of humanity's capabilities.

To honor those nameless heroes of 9/11 and the nationwide civic ethos that took hold but sadly dissipated in the aftermath of the attacks, I propose a 9/11 National Day of Service (a.k.a. Be Kind When Nobody's Looking Day). Every year on 9/11, in observance of the events of that day, each of us, at least once that day, should do something kind for somebody else and not get caught doing it.

It's as simple as that. Just do something nice. Help someone else, directly or indirectly. Then just keep it to yourself. Don't tell anyone. Just know that you did it.

That's the right tribute to the heroes of 9/11—the firemen, the co-workers who stuck together, strangers who comforted the injured and scared, the volunteers who dug for the remains. That's the right way to honor this singular moment in history where we paused, if only and regrettably too briefly, to genuinely care for each other. This is how we should remember 9/11. By doing what the heroes did. If each of us does that—even if only 10 percent of us does that—imagine what a day it will be in this country.

In support of the spirit of this observance, I propose a few simple rules:

- There will be no awards.
- There will be no corporate sponsors.
- There will be no official Twitter feed, Facebook page, or YouTube channel.
- There will be no reality show.
- There will be no party affiliation or membership required.
- There will be no official press releases and no press conference.
- There will be no film rights or television rights.

- There will be no logo.
- There can be no winner or loser.
- No score will be kept.
- It will cost the taxpayers nothing.

The opportunities to do heroic things are all around us, every day. We just need a trigger. The 9/11 National Day of Service gives us that trigger. It takes us all back to the simplest lessons of 9/11—lessons that perhaps have been all too forgotten, but shall not be if this proposed day of observance is recognized and formally enacted.

Therefore, I urge every local, state, and federal government to adopt the 9/11 National Day of Service in order to let each of us be a hero, to be that person that so many were on the day the world now knows, and will always know, as 9/11.

Being interviewed by an ABC News reporter moments after the collapse of Tower 1.

Reunited with Tina Hansen the week after the attacks.
courtesy of eric o'connell

Joy and I on our wedding day, September 13, 2002.

The Network Plus gang (minus me) outside Harpo Studios after filming
The Oprah Winfrey Show.

To: Mr. Benfante and Mr. Cerqueira
For: Saving a life

9/17/01

Dear Mr. Benfante and Mr. Cerqueira,

I am writing to you because I think it was very heroic of you to rescue that woman in the World Trade center. It was an act of bravery and unselfishness. You were very altruistic and caring. You put your lives on the line to save some one's life. That was very daring.

Love,
Elyse Lewis

One of the cards I received from the students in Mrs. Toussaint's fifth-grade class from Heights Elementary School in Sharon, Massachusetts.

Another card from Mrs. Toussaint's class.

THE WHITE HOUSE

WASHINGTON

October 31, 2001

Mr. Michael Benfante
Network Plus
601 West 26th Street
New York, New York 10001

Dear Michael,

We send you our heartfelt thanks and the thanks of a grateful Nation for your selfless efforts in responding to the tragic events of September 11.

Your actions in the midst of this national tragedy were truly heroic. Your risking your life to help carry a disabled woman down 68 floors to safety reflected the best of the American spirit. The many remarkable acts of courage, kindness, and generosity have touched and inspired our country.

May God bless you and your family, and may God bless America.

Sincerely,

Letter from President and Laura Bush.

Edward M. Kennedy

October 5, 2001

Mr. Michael Benfante
Network Plus
601 West 26th Street, 4th Floor
New York, NY 10001

Dear Michael:

I recently learned of your heroism during the terrorist attack on the World Trade Center on September 11th, 2001 and would like to take this opportunity to commend you for your bravery and valor in a time of crisis.

Your story is nothing less than courageous. Your selfless concern for others deserves recognition and the thanks and praise of all Americans. Vicki joins me in applauding you on a job well done. Your country is proud of you.

With warmest wishes,

Sincerely,

Edward M. Kennedy

Letter from Senator Ted Kennedy.

ACKNOWLEDGMENTS

I KNEW ALL ALONG I could never write this book alone. But I also never could have expected the incredible amount of support from the amazing people with whom I was blessed throughout the process. I can never say thank you enough for what they did, but I will say what I can right here to each of them.

To my coauthor, Dave "the Most Interesting Man Alive" Hollander, for without his relentless dedication, unquestionable trust, and determined commitment to the truth, this book would not have been possible. I am truly a richer person for having him in my life and for being able to call him my friend.

To my gifted team of handlers and advisers: my agent Ian Kleinert, my editor Mark Weinstein, and my sage counsel Sanford L. Hollander, Esq.

To my friends whose loyalty and ever-present encouragement steeled my determination to say what I had to say: Brian "Boozer" Wenrich, Jeff Fernandez, Scott Jenkins, Robert Finkman, Alexandra Gratsas Hollander.

To my family for their unconditional love without which I would be nowhere, silent and indifferent: Evelyn Benfante, Susan Benfante, Angelo and Lisa Benfante, Maria and Marc Guarducci, and my cousin Jimmy Giorgio.

And to the three greatest forces in my life:

My wife, Joy, for her love and support.

My son, Michael, for reminding me every day what's most important in life.

And God, for continuing to show me the way.

ABOUT THE AUTHORS

MICHAEL BENFANTE became a national hero for his actions on September 11, 2001, when he and a co-worker carried a disabled woman in a wheelchair down sixty-eight flights of stairs and out of the World Trade Center North Tower to safety, just minutes before the tower imploded. He is the recipient of a host of honors and international recognition and has testified at a U.S. Senatorial special hearing about his 9/11 experience. Benfante is a 1987 Brown University graduate. He currently lives with his wife and his son in Bloomfield, New Jersey.

DAVE HOLLANDER is an author and columnist writing on sports and social issues in national publications including *The Huffington Post, AOL Sports, SI.com*, and *Interview*. Hollander serves on the faculty for the New York University Tisch Center for Hospitality, Tourism, and Sports Management. Hollander lives in New York City with his wife and daughter. He has known Michael Benfante for fifteen years.

INDEX